FINANCING
COLLEGE
EDUCATION

FINANCING COLLEGE EDUCATION

Kenneth A. Kohl

Irene C. Kohl

HARPER & ROW, PUBLISHERS

NEW YORK

Cambridge
Hagerstown
Philadelphia
San Francisco

1817

London
Mexico City
São Paulo
Sydney

To Mother, Ivy Campbell Caistor, who maintained that
an education is one of the most valuable possessions in
life—no one can take it away from you!
To our two students, Karen and Bob, who are still struggling
to pay for their education
To Cathy and Bill Jacobsen, whose encouragement to write this
book never faltered
To Joe Vergara, our editor, who saw this book as a great
possibility for good for the students in this country
To Rev. Robert Schuller, to whom "everything is possible"

FINANCING COLLEGE EDUCATION. Copyright © 1980 by Kenneth A. Kohl and Irene
C. Kohl. All rights reserved. Printed in the United States of America. No part of this
book may be used or reproduced in any manner whatsoever without written permission
except in the case of brief quotations embodied in critical articles and reviews. For
information address Harper & Row, Publishers, Inc., 10 East 53rd Street, New York,
N.Y. 10022. Published simultaneously in Canada by Fitzhenry & Whiteside Limited,
Toronto.

FIRST EDITION

Designer: Sidney Feinberg

Library of Congress Cataloging in Publication Data

Kohl, Kenneth A
   Financing college education.
   Includes index.
   1. College costs—United States. I. Kohl,
Irene C., joint author. II. Title.
LB2337.4.K63   1980   378.3'0973   78-20172
ISBN 0-06-012427-X
ISBN 0-06-090714-2 pbk.

80 81 82 83 84 10 9 8 7 6 5 4 3 2 1

Contents

Introduction

When Irene and I left our former jobs to come to work for Princeton University, our worlds changed. As a former executive of General Motors Acceptance Corporation, I left behind a competitive, crazy job in the automobile industry. Irene left a job as editor of a magazine that was, to say the least, a "stressful" situation.

We found, in Princeton University, jobs that were a haven from corporate world jitters and editors' deadlines. Both of us knew that behind the beautiful ivy-covered walls of *Old Nassau* we had found a peaceful home where we planned to live out our lives in relative serenity.

As Financial Aid Director at Princeton, I enjoyed the one-to-one contact with the students. Irene dealt mostly with history students, many of whom were concerned about how they would pay for their continuing education at law school. The problem of paying for college loomed as a very pressing one for many of Princeton's students.

Paying for a college education was the expertise of the Financial Aid Office, of which I was Director. Half of Princeton's student body received financial aid. This fact still surprises many people who think of Ivy League colleges as the home of the wealthy students.

And not all the protests at Princeton were funny. During the Vietnam war, there were some tense moments indeed.

During my years as Financial Aid Director, I had become very concerned with the escalating cost of college and the possibility that only the rich and the very poor would be able to afford a higher education. The rich, of course, would have no difficulty in financing their children's education; the poor would get federal grants.

As for the rest, the middle-income students who make up the majority on college campuses, I came to feel that the state and federal governments should provide financial assistance so that they, too, could attend the college of their choice, whether private or state. Society benefits from higher education, so society should help in the cost of education for everyone.

At a time when approximately one out of two students was headed for college or an institution of higher learning, and virtually all these students required some kind of assistance, it became obvious that more aid had to be made available.

I came to hear more and more about the Federal Guaranteed Student Loan Program as the only hope for middle-class families that had to borrow money so their children could attend college. Since loans were not based on family income, a student could borrow money whether his or her family made $25,000 or $100,000. I had also heard that the program was in deep trouble, due to the nasty habit some students had of defaulting on their loans, declaring bankruptcy when they graduated and declining to repay. Another type of student justified nonpayment by claiming that he or she hadn't received a "meaningful education."

I had been at Princeton for five years when the director of the Federal Guaranteed Student Loan Program left. The program was foundering and a replacement was sorely needed. I was urged to consider the position and was invited to Washington to meet with the United States Commissioner of Education, John Ottina.

After much thoughtful consideration, I accepted the position, for not only was I committed to the cause of financial aid but, having a daughter of my own in college, I was experiencing personally the squeeze every middle-income family with children in college goes through. I simply couldn't let a good program die.

My first problem as director was the student defaults, which had assumed such proportions that Congress was threatening to cancel the billion-dollar program. I was summoned to testify before the Senate Subcommittee on Education, whose chairman, Senator Claiborne Pell, asked me a dozen questions about the loan program and student defaults, to which the only honest answer I could give was, "I don't know." The Senator finally asked how long I had held the position of associate commissioner for guaranteed student loans. When I replied, "Two days," the Senator laughed and directed me to return two days later with the answers to all his questions. That was my initiation to Washington.

Our biggest problem in the program was its budget. As a former credit manager at General Motors, I knew we needed to hire and train a staff to collect the defaulted loans, not from students who honestly couldn't afford to pay, but from those who simply didn't want to.

There were many who did not applaud our efforts to collect the defaulted loans. One morning at breakfast my wife gasped and handed me a page from the Washington *Post*. There, big as life, was a caricature of me as lanky Uncle Sam wringing the neck of a wretched student whose tongue was hanging down half the page. The accompanying editorial was equally unappreciative of our crusade. The *Post* made it up to me later, however, in a unique manner.

The student default rate in the District of Columbia was possibly the highest in the country. Washington banks were in fact refusing to give any more student loans. Concerned for the students thus denied the means to their education, I called Mayor Walter Washington to enlist his help. I called him for an entire week, vainly leaving urgent telephone messages to please call me back.

The newspapers had got wind of the problem of student loans in the nation's capital, and one young reporter phoned and asked me what my department was doing about it. I told him we desperately wanted to get together with Mayor Washington, but he hadn't returned my telephone calls.

The next day, the top of the *Post's* editorial page bore the statement: "Mayor Washington, please return Mr. Kohl's call so that something can be done about the default rate in the

City of Washington and the students here won't lose their Guaranteed Student Loans. Mr. Kohl wants to do something about it but he needs you to help work out the program. Pick up your telephone and call him." Needless to say, Mayor Washington quickly dispatched his commissioner for human resources and four other gentlemen to my office to work out the problem.

While in Washington I dealt with numerous such problems, the solution to which helped make it possible for many bright young people all over the country to afford college. I take pride in this, and I am confident that any student using the information in this book *can* go to college no matter what his or her family's financial resources.

—Kenneth A. Kohl

1

How Families Cope with the Escalating Cost of College

A sobering fact of life to many American families with college-age students is that, over the next four years, the cost of a four-year education at an Ivy League university could reach $36,000. As if it was not enough of a shock to the parent's pocketbook, this figure may not reflect the true cost of college, for there are many overlooked costs that do not show up in the printed budgets.

What are the costs of attending a typical Ivy League university? How do they compare with the costs of attending a typical state university? The comparative costs for two semesters (one year) are approximately these:

Expenses	State University	Ivy League
Tuition and fees	$1,000	$5,100
Room and board	1,650	2,100
Transportation	350	350
Miscellaneous	600	850
TOTAL	$3,600	$8,400

The burden of financing a college education is very real and very painful, especially for a family with several children in school at the same time. The good news is that financial aid for a college education is on the increase. Nevertheless, each family must try to cope with the financial crunch in its own way.

Here are examples of families we have counseled and how they coped with financing college education:

GARY

Gary was a young man from the ghetto. His father and mother were unemployed. Gary's dream was to attend college. At an early age, he started working after school and during summers. He saved all the money he could after contributing some to his family. When Gary received his college admission notice, he contacted the financial aid director. The director helped him with a financial aid package of job, loan and scholarship. Gary, who became a basketball star at college, finished his four years of college, going home every summer to work and contributing some of his earnings to his family.

JIMMY

I met Jane in a gift shop in a large Miami hotel where she was a clerk. We started to chat and she told me about her son Jimmy who was graduating from high school with honors. He wanted to be an engineer, but, to her deep regret, she couldn't afford to send him to college. She was divorced and earned only a small salary. Worse, she did not know how to investigate scholarships or loans.

After I outlined the Guaranteed Student Loan Program, she thanked me and indicated she would check into it immediately. The next day there was a note in my box from Jane. The bank had given her son a $2,500 Guaranteed Student Loan, which she was to receive annually. Before I left, Jimmy had received admission to a local college and was on his way to becoming an engineer.

THE JOHNS FAMILY

A serious problem families face is having two or three children of college age at the same time. Pat Johns was the mother of three such children. Because the Johnses were dedicated to educating their family, Pat took a job as an interior decorator at a New York store, and her husband, a teacher, got an additional job part time. Pat complained that they never saw each other because they were so busy working. Educating three children simultaneously was becoming a real burden. When Pat discovered that *each* child could receive a $2,500 Guaranteed Student Loan annually, the burden lifted and her husband gave up his second job.

Federal financial aid is changing constantly. In addition, new scholarships keep being introduced—such as the Clairol scholarships for displaced homemakers. It's up to you—keep informed.

MARY JONES

Mary Jones discovered that the Food Fair Stores had a fine scholarship program. She got a job as a checker at her local Pantry Pride, a Food Fair subsidiary, and worked there for two years. Now her son is being helped to go to college on a Food Fair Stores scholarship. She still works at Pantry Pride; she likes the job.

Involve your family in your dreams for a college education. The burden of financing an education is much lighter when the whole family becomes concerned.

KAREN, OUR DAUGHTER

Karen, a pretty fair artist, needed money to finance her college education. She decided to involve her parents—the authors of this book—in her dream of attending art school. Finding that there was a market for framed pictures of garden flowers, she asked her father to price picture frames and mats. He reported that they could be purchased inexpensively at a local chain variety store. Her mother helped with advertising the pictures and contacting clients. Karen found a good market for her pictures and sold quite a few over the summer. Her earnings, coupled with her Guaranteed Student Loan, amounted to sufficient funds for her first year at college. Thus not only was the whole family involved, but she had contributed her own money toward her education.

Most successful planning starts *early*. The majority of young people who come to us for counseling come with a work permit in their hands. Teenagers can, of course, get the traditional jobs as baby-sitters, gardeners, typists and waiters and waitresses. But then there are the jobs they can create for themselves.

MARY AND LIZ

Mary and Liz packed picnic lunches for people going to the shore on weekends. Their service became so popular that it developed into a full-time summer job.

RICHARD AND BOB

Richard and Bob started a summer camp for children of working mothers. In addition to the usual games, they introduced their young charges to the art of kitemaking. After the summer, they found a real market for their kites and produced enough money to help finance their college education.

Look around—what services could you provide in your community?

Some financial problems arise when parents do not contribute to their children's education. Stan was a freshman in college when a family argument erupted over finances and his parents declined to subsidize his future education. He came to us desperate, for he really wanted to finish college. We encouraged him to look into an ROTC scholarship.

The Reserve Officers' Training Corps, on hundreds of campuses across the United States, gives out hundreds of scholarships a year. A student can apply for one up to the junior year in college, and it is renewable each year. ROTC scholarships can be worth up to $32,000 for four years, depending on the college. Leadership qualities, good marks and fine recommendations are the criteria for award; both men and women are considered.

STAN

Stan was fortunate. He was selected for an ROTC scholarship which paid his tuition, room and board; he also received $100 a month for ten months.

Stan graduated as a second lieutenant and is looking forward to his career in the Army (he must serve four years).

Financing a college education is often a matter of compromise. Not everyone may be able to afford an education at a high-cost private institution. Some may have to compromise by attending a state university; others may find it necessary to attend a junior college.

There are those who will suggest that the greater cost of tuition and fees at the private institutions represents a higher level of faculty competence and smaller classes; this is not necessarily true. Faculty pay at some state universities is equal to or greater than that of some private institutions, implying that superior faculty is sought. Likewise, class sizes can be about the same.

This book is written to make you aware that *everyone* can pay for education after high school. If you are willing to *plan* for it, *save* for it, *borrow* for it and *work* for it—read on!

2

How to Choose A College Home

College is a social as well as an academic community that will be home to the student for several very important years.

How Do You Find a College to Suit Your Academic Needs and Your Social Needs?

1. Colleges and junior colleges are not all alike. You need to look at a number of colleges before you accept an offer to attend a particular one. Some people are happier in a small college than in a prestigious university.

JANE D.

Jane D., who had long dreamed of attending a famous Eastern university, wound up wishing she was back home in California. We met her at a reception to which freshmen and their families were invited to meet the university's President and members of the faculty. Jane was a pretty girl but she looked extremely unhappy. Later in the day my wife met her in the powder room. Tears streaming down her face, Jane explained that she had made a mistake and wanted to go home, but she had paid her tuition and had no money to fly to California.

My wife made an appointment for Jane to see me the next day. It was quite apparent to me that Jane was just not going to make it in the university community. Even at eighteen, she was very homesick and couldn't accept her new surroundings. I told her to speak with the dean of students; with his approval,

I would get her tuition refunded so that she could return home. Meanwhile, we had called her parents and they concurred with our decision.

As it turned out, there was no question in anyone's mind that Jane needed to go home quickly. We bought her ticket, drove her to the airport and put her on the plane, which her parents would meet on its arrival.

2. Set up a time schedule so that you can thoroughly assess a number of different colleges. It takes a considerable amount of time to get appointments and have interviews with both admissions and financial aid officers.

We always advise starting no later than your junior year—sooner, if possible—so that you have time to look at at least ten colleges.

When you particularly like a college, see if the admissions director will schedule a few days in which you can attend classes and live in a student dormitory.

Admissions offices are finding that this service is worthwhile to both the student and the university: the student assesses his chances of fitting into the college community, and the university is likely to get a happier student who adjusts with a minimum of problems.

Don't plan your visit to a campus during a break or a holiday; just looking at buildings tells you nothing about how you will fit into the social and academic life of the university.

3. If you know your field of major interest, try to get an interview with the head of that academic department. If you can, talk to some of the professors, too. This will give you an idea of how you will be treated as a student.

4. "Package yourself"—write a student autobiography. A student autobiography will not only aid you in gaining admission, it will help you compose yourself during an interview, especially if you are shy—as most of us are—at meeting new people.

ELLEN

Ellen was a particularly bright but very, very shy student who desperately wanted to be admitted to one of the prestigious women's universities. She was the only student who didn't moan when we suggested writing a student autobiography, as we do to all students whom we counsel. Anything that would help her in the admissions interview appealed to her.

She worked really hard at her student biography, incorporating her own beautiful artwork and photographs. Furthermore, she convinced her parents to visit ten colleges with her. Amazingly, she gained admission to all ten of these highly selective schools. Ellen's success with the student autobiography convinced all those who heard about it that the effort was well worth making. From then on, the students we worked with gave us little opposition when we mentioned working on a student biography.

How To Make Up a Student Autobiography

1. You can't compose a student autobiography if you don't do anything. Get involved in activities you like, even if you doubt your talent. If you are interested, join!

2. It is a good practice to record your activities as you go along. If you wait to gather your material until later, you may well have forgotten many items.

3. When the time comes to prepare your autobiography, get a binder at your local stationery store. It doesn't have to be expensive, but it should be conservative in design.

Place the following in your binder:

a. If you are in a play, note the date, place and your role. Save the playbill and include it. Record the particulars of any forensic debate you participated in.

b. If you join a team and your sport is written up in the local newspaper or your school paper, include the clipping.

c. List your interests outside school: ballet lessons, hospital volunteer work, Girl or Boy Scouting. A part-time job to help with your school expenses is especially important to note.

Colleges like well-rounded, good citizens. It's a mistake to feel that they are interested only in brilliant class presidents. If you are a good citizen in your school and community, chances are that you will be a good citizen in your college community.

d. Don't go overboard and create activities that you have never participated in. The student who wrote in his admissions application that he worked with a pygmy tribe in South Africa did stretch the imagination somewhat. At the age of seventeen, few have such opportunities.

e. Include your picture on the front page. It makes your autobiography look more professional.

f. Of course, any scholastic awards should be recorded.

g. When you put down your employment history, make sure you include:

What jobs did you have?
Where did you work?
What did you do?
How did you like your job?

Incidentally, this same approach works well for employment interviews, whether for a campus job or when you graduate.

Keep a student autobiography in college, and you will be prepared for your first job interview when you graduate.

Since a student autobiography is such a personal thing, every individual will have unique achievements to record: what have you done that hasn't been mentioned here?

When the opportunity presents itself in your admissions interview, say that you have written up a short autobiography of your achievements and hope the admissions administrator will review it.

This will give you the opportunity to compose yourself for the interview, concentrating on questions you particularly want to ask. If you are afraid you might forget them, write them down ahead of time.

Find Out About the College in an Admissions Interview

So many students worry about making a good impression in the admissions interview that they fail to ask the questions they need to ask.

Don't worry about the interview. If you have dressed in a presentable manner, have made up your student autobiography and are prepared to answer questions in a friendly, courteous manner, your interview will go well.

What Questions Should You Ask?

1. Ask about the courses you need to take to prepare you for the field you desire. Make sure there are not a lot of required "filler courses" that you are not interested in.

2. Ask about housing. In this day of coed dorms and other types of housing arrangements, you should stress the kind you would like and find out if it is available.

3. If you are especially interested in sports, ask about them. Make sure the college has facilities for any sport of particular interest to you.

4. What about social life? Ask about the kind of cultural activities that are available: the dances and mixers.

5. Most important, if you need financial aid, say so. Find out if you can schedule an interview with the financial aid director.

Often, the admissions and the financial aid offices are located near each other; admissions people will frequently introduce the student to the financial aid officer after the admissions interview is over. If the admissions people don't offer to do this, you might ask them to.

Your admissions interview can introduce you to valuable acquaintances which is helpful if you end up choosing a particular university. Look forward to it as a nice experience.

Incidentally, the more interviews you have, the more skillful you will become.

How Do You Know If You Will Fit into the Student Body?

Ask yourself the following questions to determine how well you will fit into a specific college community.

1. Is the college or educational institution of a size you could feel comfortable in?

If you are from a small town, you may not be happy in a

college that has a student body of 40,000. On the other hand, if you are bored with your small-town community, a large university with lots of activities may be just what you are looking for.

2. Are the students in an income bracket you can relate to and feel comfortable with?

3. Are there any dress codes at this university? If so, are they adhered to strictly?

Though dress codes are the exception rather than the rule these days, in some few schools they are definitely set down and adhered to rather strictly.

4. What is the morality of the college?

If you have a very high ethical code and the school has a very relaxed one, you might feel ill at ease. You will be happier with a school that has definite rules of conduct for its students.

There are many such schools in the country. If this is important to you, by all means check on it.

5. What is the geography of the college?

Do you like cold weather and skiing? Then the University of Miami might not be for you.

Will you find it difficult to adjust emotionally if you go too far from home? Look for a school you like nearby that will allow you to spend some of your weekends at home. And, if you do go far away from home, perhaps you should make sure you can afford to spend a lot of money coming home your first year in college! If you get homesick, will your parents send you the money to come home when you want to? Can they afford the long-distance telephone calls?

6. Can your parents afford this college?

This is possibly the most important question you have to ask yourself. It isn't fair to your parents to expect them to make tremendous financial sacrifices so that you can attend the college your heart desires. There may be other colleges that offer equally good academic programs at lower cost.

7. Do you want to play on a team or participate in a particular sport?

If you are really interested in sports, take a look at the athletic facilities and talk to the coaches. Ask them about your chances of participating.

Women especially, due to Title IX, now have a bigger opportunity in college athletics. Many are excelling at basketball, tennis and swimming, to mention a few. Make sure your preferred college has become adjusted to the role of women as "college athletes."

8. Do you need a job to help pay for your college expenses?

If you need a job, make sure you ascertain the availability of employment in the local community as well as on campus. (Many times college employment is available only to those in financial need.)

9. Do you love to eat well?

If the quality of food is important to you, ask some students to evaluate the food. There may be sororities or fraternities whose food surpasses the standard college fare and which admit nonmembers to their dining rooms.

Apply to at Least Ten Colleges

Don't limit your applications to a group of similar colleges. The admission standards of such schools as Princeton, Harvard, Yale and Dartmouth are usually high and usually the same. If one rejects you, chances are that they all will.

Apply to at least ten colleges of different types—private, public, community and junior colleges. (Don't forget, though, that when you are considering vocational schools advertised as guaranteeing you an immediate job, go carefully—apply all the standards you would apply to any other college. Some of these schools are fine, but some you need to be wary of.)

If your scholastic ability will not allow you to attend the prestigious four-year school you fancy, pick a good junior college, make an admirable scholastic and achievement record and reapply to your favorite college as a transfer student. Many colleges value transfer students because they have proved their ability to perform in an academic environment.

Students who choose a college solely because the buildings are beautiful or their best friend is attending it are making a serious mistake.

Your first consideration should be the quality of the education you will receive, and this may indeed be superior in a school with modest buildings and a small faculty.

Evaluate how happy you will be in the physical setting of the school you are contemplating, considering the weather, the size of the campus and the composition of the student body.

The college you choose should fit your social as well as your academic needs, so set aside enough time to visit at least six colleges to make adequate comparisons.

Don't fail to determine whether your parents can afford to send you to a particular college. No matter how much you love a school, your parents should not have to make tremendous sacrifices to finance your education there.

Since you are attending an institution of higher learning either to prepare for a particular career or to find an area of study that will lead you to the career of your choice, you must finally ask: Will the college you are considering prepare you for the career you are interested in? Are there courses available in your areas of interest if you have not decided on a particular career?

Checking all the factors we have suggested should enable you to choose the college home you will be happiest in.

3

Planning for an Education Helps Make Paying for It Easier

Even the best intentions to save enough for a college education can be thwarted by inflation, leaving parents and students angry and frustrated.

The most important objective of this book is to present the options parents and students have in paying for a college education if they start planning early!

I work with many students, and I wish I could say that most of them know what they want to do in life. That simply isn't true! When I ask them what their career goals are, I often get a smart-aleck answer—"Lying on the beach in Hawaii," for example—because they have no career goals.

Women, in particular, don't seem to be planning for their careers, despite what you may read in the papers. Even though women now constitute over 30 percent of the work force the important question is, what work are they doing?

Statistics from the U.S. Department of Labor indicate that, despite the women's movement, 90.8 percent of the lawyers and judges in America are men. Are there many women doctors or engineers? Today, 98.2 percent of all engineers and 87.2 percent of all doctors are men.

Where are the majority of women working? In the clerical fields as typists and secretaries.

Apparently women are still saying to themselves, If I don't want to work, I can always get married. No matter what the media would lead you to believe, the successful women doctors, lawyers and editors pictured in the magazines are the exception rather than the rule. This means that upward mobility and really good pay for women is still a long way off.

In Ohio, a forty-member task force of the U.S. Department of Labor studying women in the employ of the state government found that upward job mobility for these government workers was a long way off. This condition was attributed to poor guidance counseling. The survey revealed that most of the women interviewed still aspired to be office workers, technicians and teachers—fields that do not help a woman to create a meaningful salary history. The accelerating divorce rate is an indicator that women must learn to think of themselves as potential heads of houses with the necessity of making enough money to support a family on their own.

Women are entitled to guidance counseling that truly prepares them for a high-salaried career. In the absence of adequate guidance counseling at the high school level, parents can work to get better career guidance for their students.

For one thing, they can enlist their friends in various professions and careers to talk to their high school children, giving them realistic expectations.

Further, community or local civic organizations can be enlisted in a project to help fill the void left by poor guidance counseling.

A recent newspaper article told about a Junior League organization that, having decided that the schools were not encouraging young women to think about nonstereotyped careers, set up a program to encourage them to consider alternatives. First they provided the school library with books describing a variety of careers for women. Students who became interested in specific careers could obtain appointments to talk with women in these fields. The League also furnished financial counseling for each individual.

Another community, a few years back, instituted a Career Day at the local YWCA, to be attended by the young people of the area. Much publicity was given to the project in the newspaper, and many outstanding businessmen and women were asked to come and talk about their professions. There was a big turnout, mostly of boys. Few girls in this working-class community wanted to admit they were interested in anything but marriage. Yet the next year almost as many girls as boys came to Career Day, and they asked almost as many questions.

The one stumbling block in this program was the small amount of financial aid. At that time there were few federal programs. Thus scholarships were the major resource for a college education, and there simply were not enough of them to go around. Despite the obstacles to their college educations, these young people of modest background, given a chance, were interested in their careers. Career Day in this community came to be a successful annual institution.

Planning for a Career by Getting Part-time Jobs in a Field of Your Choice While in High School.

If you are in high school and need a part-time job, go out and find one in a field you are interested in. Not only will you earn money for your college education, but you will be getting valuable experience in career options.

The wise student will always have two careers in mind, so that if one doesn't work out, the other is likely to. Further, second careers come in handy to finance such mundane needs as eating and having a roof over your head. Many a Ph.D. has had to find work as a milkman because his particular field was saturated and he couldn't get a job.

We have found that some of the most prestigious colleges have the worst career counseling and some of the smallest schools have the best.

Taking the SAT Early Enables Students to Equate Scholarship with Career Goals.

It is advisable for students to take the SAT early in their junior year so they'll learn their scholastic standing. Low SAT scores may shrink your chances of getting into a prestigious school. But since this test is also a learning test which can be taken three times, most students bring up their scores appreciably. Another thing the SAT scores will tell you is your chance to qualify for an academic scholarship.

Then, too, if your SAT score is low for the career of your choice, you have time to go for another option—a career in the field you are interested in, certainly, but one that fits in with your scholastic ability.

How Good Is Your High School's Guidance Department?

Parents are generally unaware of the very great need for well-trained guidance counselors in the school system.

A parent who is going to spend thousands of dollars to finance a student's education should certainly invest a few dollars in heading him or her in the right direction. In the absence of a school counseling service, a good private counselor should be sought, one who can devote hours, not minutes, to directing the student's career.

The School System Should be Encouraged to Introduce Courses in Career Options in Junior High School.

Career options is a learning process. It can't start too early, and junior high school is not too early. Some farsighted schools have introduced these courses, but often they are discontinued when parents cry that it is too early for Johnny or Jane to think about what they want to do with their lives—they are only children!

We have found that once school systems cancel these courses they are rarely heard of again. The parents and students have lost a valuable learning tool.

What is wrong with thinking as early as junior high school about what you want to do with your life? Many people never really think seriously about this important matter, and they drift from their B.A. to their M.A. and then to their Ph.D.—still trying to find themselves.

How Can You Pay for Your Student's Career If You Don't Know What It Is?

Many students want careers that are going to be especially expensive. Late-entry careers—those that require more than four years of college, such as medicine, law and engineering—cost more than the basic education. If you know in advance that you want to get into a late-entry career, you are going to have to start saving and planning early.

SVEN JACKSON

Sven Jackson wanted to be a chemical engineer; he arrived at this decision in his senior year in high school. His parents came to us for help, very distressed. Since Mr. Jackson had an income of $35,000 and assets of $30,000, they had to pay $7,000 a year toward Sven's education, according to the financial aid form. But the Jacksons' assets were all tied up in their home, and $7,000 was out of their reach. "Let's not panic," we cautioned and then discussed the options for the Jacksons and Sven.

First we pointed out that Sven could attend a local college where the costs would be only $1,500 yearly. They decided against this; their son was a fine student, and the courses at this particular school were not right for his major. After further discussion, this family decided that a private university was the only option.

Sven was admitted to a college that cost $7,000 yearly and provided no financial aid at all. Yet Sven made it, for together we worked it out, tough as the problem appeared to be. Sven would just have to find the highest-paying summer job available to him. And he did—he found a construction laborer's job that paid $5.50 per hour.

Working forty hours a week during June, July and August, Sven made a total of $2,160. He saved $1,800. Not a bad beginning for savings from summer employment!

We met with the family again and came up with these figures:

Yearly college costs	$7,500
Sven's summer savings	1,800
Sven still needed	$5,700

Where were the Jacksons to get this kind of money before school opened?

We sent Sven out to canvass the local banks, and one of them agreed to lend Sven $1,875 yearly through the Guaranteed Student Loan Program.

Mom and Dad agreed that since he wanted the education so badly and was willing to go into debt for it ($7,500 for four years), they would pay the 7 percent interest on the loan while he was in college.

Now Sven's college financial picture looked like this:

Yearly college costs	$7,500
Summer savings	1,800
Guaranteed student loan	1,875
Sven still needed	$3,825

Next Sven visited his college to find out if there were any campus jobs he could get during school.

He applied our theory of seeking work in his own field, and he got a job in the chemistry lab for $3 per hour. This provided him with another $700, but he was still short.

Maybe he could save money on room and board. He studied the college budget data and found he could save $300 on the cost of a room by sharing an apartment with two other students off the campus. He also discovered that by eating only breakfast and dinner he could save $200 on his campus meal contract.

Finally, the college budget allowed $700 for miscellaneous expenses. Sven decided that he could budget carefully and save about $300 here. The total savings that he made from adjusting the college budget to suit his own life-style totaled $800.

Now, his available funds were $5,175 and he needed $2,325. Then his family decided that a student who could sacrifice so much deserved some help. They located a good Parents' Loan

Yearly college costs	$7,500
Summer savings	1,800
Guaranteed student loan	1,875
Still needed	$3,825
Chemistry job	$ 700
Savings—room	300
Savings—meals	200
Savings—miscellaneous expense	300
Final need	$2,325

Program that enabled them to pay the additional $2,325 Sven needed yearly. The Jacksons would be paying $1,200 yearly, plus interest, for eight years.

Much as we admire this family's endeavors in enabling a student to attend the college of his choice, we must point out that they would have saved themselves much effort if they had started planning early!

Planning for an education helps make paying for it easier! If you haven't planned ahead and discover that you need money, you may find you need to borrow large sums from various sources.

Funds are available, but sacrifices will have to be made.

Some of the ways of finding money to provide for the cost of college are:

1. Various student and parent loan programs.
2. Scholarships.
3. On-campus and off-campus employment.
4. Summer employment.
5. Attending a state school or any institution that costs less.
6. Sharing living space and budgeting carefully for food and miscellaneous expenses.

4

Make a Friend of Your College's Financial Aid Officer

TOM F.

Tom F. lived in a little town in New Jersey where he was a junior in a large regional high school. Since he was an average student, he didn't qualify for many of the scholarships that stressed scholastic ability.

His family earned only $15,000 a year, so he *could* qualify for financial aid. And he had a twin brother, Allen, who would be attending college at the same time.

Tom made an appointment with his guidance counselor. He needed to know what schools might be best for him; how much they would cost; what the scholastic requirements were; and how to apply for admission and financial aid.

His guidance counselor advised Tom to apply to different types of colleges—private, state and two-year. She further recommended that he start early in applying for financial aid.

Not only did she advise him to apply to the state for financial aid, but she suggested he look into some local scholarships that were awarded on the basis of financial need rather than academic excellence. She recommended that Tom start visiting the colleges he was interested in, going to both the admissions office and the financial aid office. The financial aid officer, she said, could give Tom a reasonably accurate idea of how much it would cost to attend the university. Further, she encouraged him to look over the many college catalogues in her office.

Tom pored over the catalogues and found quite a few colleges he was interested in. One in particular caught his eye. In the financial aid section of the catalogue for Fairleigh Dickinson College in Madison, New Jersey, there was an outline of a family plan.

He made an appointment with the financial aid director of Fairleigh Dickinson, who told him at their interview that it was a financial aid plan that was *not* based on financial need.

Under the terms of this plan, she explained, if Tom attended the college full time (taking at least 12 credit hours), he could be the sponsor student for any other member of his family who wished to attend. He would pay full tuition, but the other family member would pay only half tuition, depending on the number of credits taken. (The sponsoring student must also be a *dependent* student, as defined by IRS regulations.)

Tom and his brother applied and were accepted at Fairleigh Dickinson, where Allen now pays only half tuition.

Tom and Allen had followed their guidance counselor's advice and filled out all the financial aid forms. Thus they received a federal grant, the Basic Educational Opportunity Grant. Further, they found they could commute from home to Fairleigh Dickinson, thereby avoiding the cost of room and board.

You see how starting early and taking the initiative for finding your own financial aid can help ease your family's concern and frustration. And how important it is to make your guidance counselor and your financial aid officer your friends.

What You Can Learn from Financial Counseling.

One of the most important contributions of the financial aid officer is financial counseling. You might be asked: Could you live on a budget? Do you have a tendency to spend beyond your means? You might be told to keep a diary listing everything you spend each day. Financial aid officers are people knowledgeable not only in financial counseling but in financial aid resources (federal and state as well as university). They control all funds the college provides.

The financial aid office can give you a reasonably accurate projection of how much it will cost you to attend that university. If you are going to live on campus, it is a good time to realize what your expenses will be. Maybe you thought you couldn't afford to attend—but it might cost less than you think!

Thus your first question to the financial aid officer should be:

1. *How Much Will It Cost Me to Attend This University?*

Here is an example of a college budget the financial aid officer might give you:

Tuition	$ 800
Fees	100
Room	900
Board (20 meals weekly)	1,400
Miscellaneous (books, laundry, etc.)	700
Travel (one round trip each semester)	150
TOTAL	$4,050

Of course, a commuting student would be able to eliminate room and board—while adding the amount it will cost to travel to and from home—over and above tuition, fees and books.

2. *I Have Often Heard About Financial Need. Exactly What Is Financial Need?*

The financial aid officer will tell you that financial need is an estimate of the cost of attending the college less the amount the student and the student's family can contribute toward that cost. For example:

The student's family can be expected to pay	$2,000
The student can save from summer employment	600
The amount available from the student's assets	200
TOTAL	$2,800

Let us assume that the college budget is $4,050. If you reduce that by the family contribution, $2,800, you will arrive at the student's financial need—$1,240.

3. *What If I Have Not Saved the Standard Required Summer Savings?*

The answers differ among financial aid offices. One office may replace the missing summer savings through a loan. Another office may require that the family pay the amount the student was unable to secure.

If the student in the example above did not save anything over the summer, the family would have to pay an additional $600. Can your family afford this?

4. *What Is My Obligation As a Student to Contribute to the Cost of My College Education?*

Students who need financial aid are expected to contribute toward the cost of their education in three ways:

A student should have earnings from a summer job—$600 is the amount freshmen students should aim for.

A student is usually expected to work approximately ten to twelve hours a week on campus while attending classes. Jobs are usually offered as a part of financial aid packages.

Loans are also commonly offered as part of a financial aid award package. Since loans have to be paid back after graduation, you should find out exactly how much you will be asked to borrow over your undergraduate career and what the payments will be when you graduate.

5. *What Is a Financial Aid Package?*

Universities award to the student a group—or "package"—of different types of financial aid. Usually, financial aid offers will include a campus job, a loan and a scholarship.

Universities generally adhere to a self-help threshold. In other words, before you receive a scholarship, you must first receive a job and a loan. Thus students with financial need may receive only a job and a loan.

Student with a $4,050 Financial Need

Employment	$ 600
Loan	1,400
Scholarship	2,050
TOTAL	$4,050

Student with a $2,000 Financial Need

Employment	$ 600
Loan	1,400
TOTAL	$2,000

6. What Other Financial Contributions Is a Student Expected to Make Toward College Costs?

Those who receive veterans' benefits from the Veterans Administration, social security benefits or gifts from relatives and friends are expected to apply those sums toward the cost of their education. All these sources are considered in arriving at the "family contribution."

7. What If I Receive a Scholarship from an Outside Source After I Am Notified of My Financial Aid Award?

If any extra resources become available to students after they receive a financial aid award, the college will usually revise its award to take into account the change of circumstances.

It is important to know that each college treats these changes differently. Some will use the outside scholarship to replace the scholarship given by the college. Other colleges will use outside scholarships to replace the job or loan portion of the initial award. Replacing a job means that you can work less—and study more. And if you borrow less, it will be easier to repay your loan. The way a college uses your outside scholarship will often affect your choice of college. To explain that, we will compare three financial aid packages at College A, College B and College C, at each of which the costs are $4,050.

College A provides a $4,050 financial aid package:

Job	$ 600
Loan	1,000
University scholarship	2,450
TOTAL AID	$4,050

College B reduces its scholarship offer because you got an outside scholarship of $1,000:

Job	$1,000
Loan	1,000
Outside scholarship	1,000
University scholarship	1,050
TOTAL AID	$4,050

College C reduces job and loan by the amount of any outside scholarship:

Job	None
Loan	$ 600
Outside scholarship	1,000
University scholarship	2,450
TOTAL AID	$4,050

Here the job is replaced by the scholarship and the loan is reduced.

Obviously, you must find out how the university is going to treat an outside scholarship before you enroll. This is especially important in the case of a large outside scholarship.

8. *What If I Want to Get My Education As an Independent Student Without the Support of My Parents?*

When a student is judged "independent," only that student's income is considered in estimating financial need; parental income is not taken into consideration.

Federal and state governments as well as all universities are very cautious in this area, since parents who can afford to educate their children might try to get them declared "independent" in order to save money.

One college catalogue makes this statement concerning the continuation of family support: "The University assumes that families of undergraduates will continue their financial support of the student throughout the undergraduate years, according to their ability to pay, as determined by the standards of the College Scholarship Service System. Should parents discontinue their financial support for reasons other than ability to pay, it is not possible for the university to accept the parental responsibility for financial support of the student. The Student Aid budget is not sufficient to allow the University to replace the parents' normal contribution with university funds."

In short, if you are not judged "independent" when you enter the college, you will not be judged "independent" after your initial aid offer is provided.

Before you enroll, find out the college's policy concerning "independent" students if you anticipate that you may have to proceed in this direction. Otherwise, you may have no option but to leave the college of your choice when you are refused "independent" status.

9. If I Get Married While Attending College, Will This Change My Financial Aid Eligibility?

Married students are as eligible for financial aid as single students. However, the financial help offered is generally limited to the amount that would be received by a single student. Parents of married students are usually asked to file financial aid forms just as though the students were unmarried.

10. What "Needs Analysis System" Does the College Use?

Most colleges use one of two analysis systems—the College Scholarship Service or the American College Testing Service. It is important to learn which of these services your college uses so that you can file the proper form to get financial aid.

This information can be obtained from the college catalogue or the high school guidance office, or by writing to the college.

The College Scholarship Service's Financial Aid Form and the American College Testing Service's Family Financial Statement are available at your high school or college.

There may be other questions that occur to you or that have been bothering you or your parents. Your visit to the financial aid office is the time to bring them out in the open and get them cleared up.

The financial aid officer will be as happy to talk with your parents as with you; suggest to your parents that they get an appointment to talk with the financial aid officer.

One recent hot summer day at Rutgers University, I was staring at a mound of papers, all crying to be worked upon, when I heard a knock at my door.

My secretary seemed to be out, so I went to the door and was greeted by a middle-aged couple with the harried look of concerned parents. I invited them into my office and inquired about their problem.

It seemed that their son was planning to attend Rutgers in the fall, and they were worried about how they were going to pay for his education. The couple earned $25,000 a year. Thus they certainly didn't qualify for financial aid at Rutgers, and they had not applied for aid, but they didn't have enough money to pay for their son's education. Could I help them?

The answer was, of course!

Since they were able to make small monthly payments, I told them about the Parent's Loan Plan that was currently available. They could get this loan in time to pay their son's college expenses.

Also, their son was quite willing to borrow, if funds were available. I directed him to his local bank and the State Guaranteed Student Loan Program, which lends directly to the student without parents having to co-sign.

Finally, I suggested that their son get summer employment and later find a job on campus in the fall.

These sources were enough to meet the student's college expenses.

As harried as financial aid officers often are, they are compassionate about the problems parents and students face in financing the escalating costs of attending college. Your financial aid officer can be a very helpful friend indeed.

5

What Is the State of Your State's Scholarship Programs?

In a recent Gallup Youth Survey, 75 percent of U.S. teenagers in high school stated that they planned to attend college. Among teenagers from white-collar families, that figure was 87 percent.

With such a large percentage of students seeking financial aid to help them achieve their education, what are the states doing to help them?

Actually, state scholarship funds have increased at a rapid rate since 1970, from $199 million in that year to almost $750 million in 1978.

One of the most progressive states in helping students overcome financial barriers to their education and giving them wider choices among schools is New York, which in 1974 established a Tuition Assistance Program.

Under TAP, in 1978–1979 New York State will make payments totaling about $244 million to 350,000 students. These awards range from $200 to $1,800 per year. There is no competition for TAP grants. Further, students may use their TAP grants in more than three hundred public and independent schools and colleges in New York.

How Do You Apply for a New York State TAP Award?

The Student Payment Application is mailed annually to all New York State high school seniors who have applied for the New York Regents Scholarship examination.

Applications are also available from your high school guidance counselor or your college financial aid officer.

You can also apply to the New York State Higher Education Services Corporation, Tower Building, Empire State Plaza, Albany, NY 12255.

1. Fill out your application carefully and make sure it's complete. Otherwise, your award will be delayed. If you do not understand a question on the application, check with your high school adviser.

2. The application should be mailed in the spring. You must apply each year for your TAP award. The amount of the award is redetermined each year.

The Student Payment Application is also used for the award of Regents College Scholarships, Regents Nursing Scholarships and other grants, such as Child-of-Veteran Awards.

3. You can get a TAP award through four years of full-time study or five years of full-time study in certain approved five-year programs.

If you complete an undergraduate degree and go on to graduate or professional study, you may again be eligible for TAP as a full-time student on the graduate level.

You may receive a total of up to eight years of TAP payments for undergraduate and graduate study.

Who Is Eligible for a TAP Grant?

Eligibility for a TAP award is based on financial need and the following qualifications:

1. Applicant must be a resident of New York State for one year prior to the first term in college.

2. Applicant must be a U.S. citizen or a permanent resident alien or paroled refugee.

3. Applicant must be matriculated in an approved program in New York State.

4. Applicant must study full time the equivalent of 12 credit hours a semester or 8 credits a quarter.

5. Applicant must be charged tuition, exclusive of fees, of $200 a year or more.

6. Applicant must file a Student Payment Application by March 21.

7. Applicant must have a family income that does not exceed the eligibility limits listed below.

The following table shows typical annual TAP awards 1978–1979 for students dependent on their parents, as well as for financially independent married students.

Income	Independent Colleges	SUNY/CUNY*	Community Colleges
$ 2,750	$1,800	$775	$700
4,000	1,725	700	625
6,000	1,595	575	495
8,000	1,455	430	355
10,000	1,295	270	200
12,000	1,115	200	200
14,000	915	200	200
16,000	675	200	200
18,000	415	200	200
20,000	200	200	200
20,000 +	0	0	0

* SUNY—State University of New York; CUNY—City University of New York.
NOTE: After the first two years of study, the awards are reduced by $200 in most cases.

The state of New Jersey has been operating a scholarship program since 1959 which now makes available:
1. New Jersey Tuition Aid Grants
2. New Jersey State Scholarships
3. New Jersey Educational Opportunity Grants
4. Guaranteed Student Loans.

New Jersey's Rules for Eligibility are Similar to Those of Other States

1. Students must be residents of New Jersey for at least twelve consecutive months prior to receiving an award. Students who are not citizens of the United States must have established permanent residency in New Jersey for at least twelve consecutive months prior to receiving an award and, according to the Immi-

gration and Naturalization Service, must have permanent resident status.

2. Students must be enrolled, or intend to be enrolled, as full-time undergraduate students at an eligible institution. Business schools, technical institutes and vocational schools are not eligible institutions. Students presently in college must, by institutional standards, maintain good academic standing.

3. Students must show evidence of financial need by filing a complete and accurate New Jersey Financial Aid Form.

4. Students who apply for renewal of a state grant must have received less than four full years of payment on the grant.

5. Students cannot be enrolled in a program of study that will lead to a degree in divinity or theology.

6. Students applying for state scholarships must present a record of high academic achievement.

7. Students who apply for an Equal Opportunity Fund Grant must be educationally and economically disadvantaged.

Do You Know How to Look for Scholarship Money in Your State?

We find that many students don't know where to look for money for scholarships in their own state.

If your high school guidance counselor can't supply you with information, use the list that follows. Write as early as you can to learn what's available.

A Directory of State Agencies of Higher Education

Alabama
Alabama Student Assistance Program
One Court Square, Suite 221
Montgomery, AL 36104
  Tel: 205: 832–6555
    Tom A. Roberson, Coordinator
    John F. Porter, Executive Director

Alaska
Alaska Department of Education
Pouch F Spate Office Building

Juneau, AK 99811
   Tel: 907: 465–2855
      Dr. Kerry Romesburg, Executive Director

Arizona
   Arizona Commission for Postsecondary Education
   1650 Alameda Drive, Suite 115
   Tempe, AZ 85028
      Tel: 602: 271–3109
         Dr. I. Don Bell, Executive Director
         Dr. R. R. Erbschloe, Assistant Director

Arkansas
   Department of Higher Education
   1301 West Seventh Street
   Little Rock, AR 72201
      Tel: 501: 371–1441 ex. 23
         Estella Williams, Coordinator of Student Aid
         Dr. M. Olin Cook, Director

California
   California Student Aid Commission
   1410 Fifth Street
   Sacramento, CA 95814
      Tel: 916: 445–0880
         Arthur S. Marmaduke, Director
         Dortha L. Morrison, Deputy Director
         Peter D. Prentiss, Scholarship Program Supervisor
         Rod Tarrer, College Opportunity Grant Program Supervisor

Colorado
   Colorado Commission on Higher Education
   1550 Lincoln Street, Room 210
   Denver, CO 30203
      Tel: 303: 892–2723
         Ms. Lindsay Baldner, Student Services Director
         Eugene B. Wilson, Executive Director

Connecticut
   Board of Higher Education for the State Student
   Financial Assistance Commission
   P.O. Box 1320
   Hartford, CT 06101
      Tel: 203: 566–2618

Dr. Romeo J. Bernier, Associate Director
John J. Siegrist, Associate in Higher Education
Patricia E. Buckland, Associate in Higher Education
Carl Mercier, Associate in Higher Education

Delaware
State Department of Public Instruction
Townsend Building
Dover, DE 19901
Tel: 302: 678–4620
Harry M. Peyser, State Specialist
School Federal Regulations and
Scholarship Programs

District of Columbia
Government of the District of Columbia
Educational Services Division
1329 East Street, N.W., Suite 1023
Washington, D.C. 20004
Tel: 202: 347–5905
Ms. Eloise Turner, Chief

Florida
Florida Student Financial Assistance Commission
Knott Building, Room 563
Tallahassee, FL 32304
Tel: 904: 487–1800
Ernest E. Smith, Administrator
Don Smading, Coordinator, Financial Aid Programs
Jensen Audioun, Coordinator, Collections and Internal Support
Blair Shuford, Florida Insured Student Loans

Georgia
Georgia Higher Education Assistance Authority
9 LaVista Perimeter Park, Suite 110
2187 Northlake Parkway
Tucker, GA 30084
Tel: 404: 393–7108
Don Payton, Executive Director
Robert McCants, Director, Student Services Division
Ruth McAdams, Supervisor, Scholarship and Grants Section
Ralph Roberts, Director, Fiscal Affairs Division

Hawaii
> State Postsecondary Education Commission
> 210 Bachman Hall
> 2444 Dole Street
> Honolulu, HI 96822
>> Tel: 808: 948–6625
>>> Fujio Matsuda, Administrative Officer

Idaho
> Office of the State Board of Higher Education
> Len B. Jordan Building, Room 307
> 650 W. State Street
> Boise, ID 83720
>> Tel: 208: 384–2270
>>> Milton Small, Executive Director
>>> Steve Xeto, Chief Fiscal Officer
>>> Delia McManus, Scholarship Officer

Illinois
> Illinois State Scholarship Commission
> 102 Wilmot Road
> Deerfield, IL 60015
>> Tel: 312: 945–1500
>>> Dr. Joseph D. Boyd, Executive Director
>>> Ralph Godzicki, Assistant Executive Director, Fiscal Affairs and Administration
>>> James A. Eanes, Director of Student Grant Programs
>>> Carol Wennerdahl, Director of State Student Loan Programs
>>> William Hilton, Director of Informational Services

Indiana
> State Student Assistance Commission of Indiana
> EDP Building, 2nd Floor
> 219 North Senate Avenue
> Indianapolis, IN 46204
>> Tel: 317: 633–5445
>>> James E. Sunday, Executive Secretary
>>> Mary Atkins Currie

Iowa
> Iowa Higher Education Facilities Commission
> 201 Jewett Building
> 9th and Grant

Des Moines, IA 50309
 Tel: 515: 281–3501
  Willie Ann Wolff, Executive Director
  Gary Nichols, Director, Student Aid Programs
  Betty J. Johnson, Administrative Assistant, Student Aid Programs
  Charles Irvin, Administrative Assistant, Student Aid Programs

Kansas
 Board of Regents—State of Kansas
 1100 Merchants National Bank Tower
 Topeka, KA 66612
  Tel: 913: 296–4827
   Dr. Gerald R. Bergen, Student Assistance Officer

Kentucky
 Kentucky Higher Education Assistance Authority
 691 Teton Trail
 Frankfort, KY 40601
  Tel: 502: 564–7990
   Paul P. Borden, Executive Director
   Marleen B. Ingle, Deputy Director, Grants

Louisiana
 Louisiana Higher Education Assistance Commission
 P.O. Box 44127, Capitol Station
 Baton Rouge, LA 70804
  Tel: 504: 389–5491
   Richard W. Petrie, Executive Director
   Mrs. Billie R. Ritter, Executive Assistant

Maine
 Division of Higher Education Services
 State Department of Educational and Cultural Services
 State Education Building
 Augusta, ME 04333
  Tel: 207: 289–2541
   Harold M. Grodinsky, Coordinator of Student Aid Programs
   Wayne E. Ross, Director, Division of Higher Education

Maryland
 State Scholarship Board
 2100 Guilford Avenue, Room 205
 Baltimore, MD 21218

Tel: 301: 383–4097
Dr. E. Kenneth Shook, Executive Director

Massachusetts
Massachusetts Board of Higher Education
Park Square Building, Room 632
31 St. James Avenue
Boston, MA 02116
Tel: 617: 727–5366
Graham R. Raylor, Vice-Chancellor for Student Affairs

Michigan
Michigan Department of Education
P.O. Box 30008
Lansing, MI 48909
Tel: 517: 373–3394
Ronald J. Jursa, Director, Student Financial Aid
Aaron Hall, Assistant Director

Minnesota
Minnesota Higher Education Coordinating Board
Capitol Square Building, Suite 901
555 Cedar Street
St. Paul, MN 55101
Tel: 512: 296–5715
Margaret Dean, Coordinator of State Scholarship and Grant Programs

Mississippi
Governor's Office of Job Development and Training
(SSIG only)
P.O. Box 4300
Jackson, MS 39216
Tel: 601: 981–2635
J. H. McMinn, Executive Director
Mrs. JoAnne Jordan, Administrative Assistant

Missouri
Missouri Department of Higher Education
600 Clark Avenue
Jefferson City, MO 65101
Tel: 314: 751–3940
Richard Stillwagon, Acting Director of Financial Aid Program
Dr. J. Bruce Roberson, Commissioner
Dr. Robert Jacobs, Assistant Commissioner for Student Affairs
Donald T. Lindenbusch, Deputy Commissioner for Fiscal Affairs

Montana
Office of the Commissioner of Higher Education
33 South Last Chance Gulch
Helena, MT 59601
Tel: 406: 449–3024
William J. Lannan, Deputy Commissioner, Planning and Research
Dr. Lawrence K. Pettit, Commissioner of Higher Education

Nebraska
Nebraska Coordinating Commission for Postsecondary Education
301 Centennial Hall South
P.O. Box 95005
Lincoln, NE 68509
Tel: 402: 471–2847
Mrs. Kathryn E. Hayes, Administrative Assistant

Nevada
Chancellor's Office
405 Marsh Avenue
Reno, NV 89509
Tel: 407: 784–4901
Mary Lou Moser, Budget and Research Analyst
Neil D. Humphrey, Chancellor

New Hampshire
Postsecondary Education Commission
66 South Street
Concord, NH 03301
Tel: 603: 271–2555
Ronald Wilson, State Financial Assistant Coordinator
Dr. James Busselle, Executive Director

New Jersey
Department of Higher Education
225 West State Street
Trenton, NJ 08625
Tel: 609: 292–8770
Dr. Haskell Rhett, Assistant Chancellor for Student Assistance and Special Programs
Dr. Elizabeth L. Ehart, Director, New Jersey State Scholarship Commission
Hubert A. Thomas, Associate Director, New Jersey State Scholarship Commission

New Mexico
Board of Educational Finance
Legislative-Executive Building, Room 201
Santa Fe, NM 67503
  Tel: 505: 827–2115
    Dr. Robert E. Rhodes, Academic Coordinator
    Dr. Robert A. Huff, Executive Secretary
    Tom Wilson

New York
New York State Higher Education Services Corporation
Tower Building
Empire State Plaza
Albany, NY 12255
  Tel: 518: 474–5592
    Eileen D. Dickinson, President
    Michael O'Shea, Executive Vice President
    Michael P. Cruskie, Vice President
    Peter Keitel, Vice President
    Lawrence O'Toole, Counsel
    Francis Hynes, Director of Administration

North Carolina
North Carolina State Education Assistance Authority
Box 2688, University Square, West
Chapel Hill, NC 27514
  Tel: 919: 929–2136
    Stan C. Broadway, Executive Director
    College Foundation, Inc.
    1307 Glenwood Avenue
    Raleigh, NC 27605
    Mr. Duffy L. Paul, Executive Director

North Dakota
North Dakota Student Financial Assistance Agency
State Capitol, 10th Floor
Bismarck, ND 58505
  Tel: 701: 224–2960
    Clark J. Wold, Director

Ohio
Ohio Board of Regents, Student Assistance Office
30 East Broad Street
Columbus, OH 43215

Tel: 614: 466–7420
  Charles W. Seward III, Director
  Tom Rudd, Assistant Director

Oklahoma
Oklahoma State Regents for Higher Education
500 Education Building
State Capitol Complex
Oklahoma City, OK 73105
  Tel: 405: 521–2444
    Johnnie M. Hopkins, Assistant Director, Student Assistance Division
    Walter M. Williams, Director, Student Assistance Division
    Dr. E. T. Dunlap, Chancellor

Oregon
Oregon State Scholarship Commission
1445 Willamette Street
Eugene, OR 37401
  Tel: 503: 686–4166
    Jeffrey M. Lee, Executive Director
    Gary K. Weeks, Deputy Director
    Tom Turner, Director, Special Programs
    James Renton, Director, Loan Program
    Floyd Bard, Director, Grant Programs

Pennsylvania
Pennsylvania Higher Education Assistance Agency
Towne House
Harrisburg, PA 17102
  Tel: 717: 737–1937
    Kenneth R. Reeher, Executive Director
    Thomas R. Fabian, Executive Deputy Director
    Earl R. Fielder, Director, Research and Plans
    Gary D. Smith, Deputy Director, Grant Program
    Samuel J. Johnson, Deputy Director, Federal and Special Affairs

Rhode Island
Rhode Island Department of Education
Office of Student Assistance
Roger Williams Building, Room 202
22 Hayes Street
Providence, RI 02908
  Tel: 401: 277–2050
    John P. Mandryk, Coordinator
    Thomas C. Schmidt, Commissioner of Education

South Carolina
  South Carolina Tuition Grants Agency
  411 Keenan Building
  Columbia, SC 29201
    Tel: 803: 758–7070
      R. Laine Ligon, Director

South Dakota
  Department of Education and Cultural Affairs
  State Capitol, Office of the Secretary of Education
  Pierre, SD 57501
    Tel: 605: 224–3119
      Dr. Ronald Reed, Secretary of the Department
      Ms. Beth Christie, Secretary

Tennessee
  Tennessee Student Assistance Corporation
  707 Main Street
  Nashville, TE 37206
    Tel: 615: 741–1346
      Kenneth Barber, Executive Director
      Howard T. Wall, Assistant Director

Texas
  Student Services Division
  Coordinating Board
  Texas College and University System
  P.O. Box 12788
  Capitol Station
  Austin, TX 78711
    Tel: 512: 475–4147
      Mack C. Adams, Head, Student Services Division
      Jane Innis, Director, Grant Programs

Utah
  Utah System of Higher Education
  University Club Building, Room 1201
  136 East South Temple
  Salt Lake City, UT 34111
    Tel: 801: 533–5617
      Harden Eyring, Assistant Commissioner, Director of Planning
      Dr. Terrell H. Bell, Commissioner

Vermont
Vermont Student Assistance Corporation
Five Burlington Square
Burlington, VT 05401
  Tel: 802: 658–4530
    Ronald J. Iverson, Executive Director
    Donald Vickers, Director of Administration
    Herbert M. Kingsland, Jr., Controller
    Donald Bernier, Director of Grant Program
    Paula Reeder, Director of Loan Program
    Timothy C. Wick, Director of Talent Search

Virginia
State Council of Higher Education
700 Fidelity Building
9th and Main Streets
Richmond, VA 23219
  Tel: 804: 786–3051
    Barry M. Dorsey, Coordinator
    Dr. Sharon Bob, Associate Coordinator, Federal Programs & Planning
    Dr. Gordon K. Davies, Director

Washington
Council for Postsecondary Education
Division of Student Financial Aid
908 East Fifth
Olympia, WA 98504
  Tel: 206: 753–3571
    Carl C. Donovan, Deputy Coordinator
    Patrick M. Callan, Executive Coordinator
    Linda LaMar, Director, Program Development
    Lew E. Dibble, Director, Internal Operations

West Virginia
West Virginia Board of Regents
West Virginia Higher Education Grant Program
950 Kanawha Boulevard, East
Charleston, WV 25301
  Tel: 304: 348–0112
    John F. Thralls, Director of Student Services
    Robert E. Long, Financial Aid Coordinator
    Jack L. Toney, Scholarship Administrator

Wisconsin
State of Wisconsin Higher Educational Aids Board
Division of Student Support
150 East Gilman Street
Madison, WI 53703
Tel: 608: 266–2897
Richard H. Johnston, Administrator
Donovan K. Fowler, Assistant Administrator

Wyoming
Wyoming Higher Education Council
1720 Carey Avenue
Cheyenne, WY 82002
Tel: 307: 777–7763
Dr. Fred Black, Executive Director

Territories

American Samoa
Department of Education
Pago Pago
American Samoa 96799
Tel: Overseas Operator 633–5237
Sala E. Samiu, Administrator of Scholarship Program

Guam
Board of Regents
University of Guam
P.O. Box EX
Agana, GU 96910
Tel: 671: 734–9258
Dr. Rosa Roberto Carter, Executive Secretary
José S. Leon Guerrero, Jr., Financial Assistance Programs

Puerto Rico
University of Puerto Rico
Central Administration
G.P.O. Box 4984–G
San Juan, PR 00936
Tel: 809: 765–6590
Eduardo Bermudez Davila, Coordinator Financial Aid Programs

Trust Territory
    Student Assistance Office
    Headquarters Department of Education
    Saipan, Mariana Islands 96950
      Tel: Saipan 9870
        Victor Hobson, Acting Student Assistance Officer
        Mrs. Toni Tell, Scholarship Officer

Virgin Islands
    Virgin Islands Department of Education
    P.O. Box 630—Charlotte Amalie
    St. Thomas, VI 00801
      Tel: 809: 774–0100
        Dr. Gwendolyn E. Kean, Commissioner
        Dr. Rehenia A. Gabrial, Director, Pupil Personnel Service

What Amounts Are Available for Scholarships in Your State?

It is important to know how much money is available in scholarships in your state so that you can determine your chances of receiving a state award.

For instance, Alaska had only $141,000 in scholarship money in 1977–1978, while California had $78,964,000. If you were a student in Alaska, your chances of receiving an award might thus have been less than if you were a student in California.

Another state that offered relatively small amounts in state scholarships was Alabama, which in 1977–1978 had $541,000, as compared to $78,103,000 in Illinois. Wyoming had only $56,000 in scholarship money, while the newer territory of the Virgin Islands had $487,000.

A student in New York State was indeed fortunate, as this state apportioned $229,400,000 to scholarships.

A DIRECTORY OF FUNDS AVAILABLE FOR SCHOLARSHIPS IN THE STATES AND TERRITORIES IN 1977–1978

Alabama
Student Assistance Program $ 541,000

Alaska
Scholarships   141,000

Arizona
State Student Incentive Grant Program   1,400,000

Arkansas
State Scholarship Program   650,000

California
State Scholarship Program   55,874,000
College Opportunity Grants   20,377,000
Occupational Education and Training Grants   2,713,000
    All programs   78,964,000

Colorado
Student Grants   8,322,000
Student Incentive Grants   1,572,000
    All programs   9,894,000

Connecticut
State Scholarship Program   2,000,000
State Supplemental Grant Program   834,000
Higher Education Grant Program   380,000
Contracted Student/Independent Colleges   3,600,000
    All programs   6,814,000

Delaware
Higher Education Scholarships   200,000
Student Incentive Grants Program   320,000
    All programs   520,000

District of Columbia
Grants   873,000

Florida
Student Assistance Grants   8,290,000

Georgia
Incentive Scholarship Program   2,807,000

Hawaii
Incentive Grant Program   484,000

Idaho
    Incentive Grant Program   388,000

Illinois
    Monetary Award Program   78,103,000

Indiana
    State Scholarships   13,500,000
    Educational Grants   4,000,000
    Freedom of Choice Grants   2,600,000
        All programs   20,100,000

Iowa
    Scholarship Program   600,000
    Tuition Grant Program   10,722,000
    Vocational/Technical Tuition Grant Program   300,000
        All programs   11,622,000

Kansas
    State Scholarships   520,000
    Tuition Grants   3,890,000
        All programs   4,410,000

Kentucky
    State Grants   3,514,000

Louisiana
    Student Incentive Grants   559,000

Maine
    Tuition Equalization Program   659,000
    Vocational/Technical Program   71,000
        All programs   730,000

Maryland
    General State Scholarships   2,117,000

Massachusetts
    General Scholarship Program   14,285,000
    Nursing Scholarships   140,000
    Special Education Scholarships   15,000
    Consortium Scholarships   150,000
    Private Non-Degree Tuition Program   95,000
        All programs   14,685,000

Michigan
     Competitive Scholarships   14,112,000
     Tuition Grants   13,700,000
          All programs   27,812,000

Minnesota
     State Scholarship Program   7,434,000
     State Grant Program   14,749,000
          All programs   22,183,000

Mississippi
     Student Incentive Grant Program   1,044,000

Missouri
     Grant Program   7,175,000

Montana
     Student Incentive Grant Program   339,000

Nebraska
     Student Incentive Grant Program   74,500

Nevada
     Student Incentive Grant Program   200,000

New Hampshire
     Incentive Program   414,000

New Jersey
     Competitive Scholarships   6,700,000
     Incentive Grants   2,400,000
     Tuition Aid Grants   4,800,000
     Country College Graduate Scholarships   200,000
     Educational Opportunity Fund Grants   10,845,000
     Public Tuition Aid Grants   4,032,000
          All programs   28,977,000

New Mexico
     Incentive Grants   561,000

New York
     Tuition Assistance Program   208,000,000
     Regents Scholarships   21,400,000
          All programs   229,400,000

North Carolina
Student Incentive Grants   2,580,000

North Dakota
Student Financial Assistance Program   343,000

Ohio
Instructional Grants   29,144,000

Oklahoma
Tuition and Grants   1,763,000

Oregon
Need Grant   4,263,000
Cash Award   350,000
    All programs   4,613,000

Pennsylvania
Higher Education Grant Program   70,936,000

Rhode Island
State Scholarships   2,092,000
Nursing Education Scholarships   40,000
Business Education Teachers Scholarships   10,000
War Orphans Scholarships   3,000
Need-Based Awards   652,000
    All programs   2,797,000

South Carolina
Tuition Grants   8,948,000

South Dakota
Student Incentive Grant Program   236,000

Tennessee
Student Assistance Awards   3,050,000

Texas
Tuition Equalization Grants   12,308,000
Student Incentive Grants   1,848,000
Public Education Grants   2,664,000
    All programs   16,820,000

Utah
    Student Incentive Grants   1,247,000

Vermont
    Incentive Grant Program   3,176,000

Virginia
    College Scholarship Assistance Program   2,488,000

Washington
    Need Grants   4,950,000

West Virginia
    Higher Education Grants   2,699,000

Wisconsin
    Higher Education Grants   12,912,000
    Tuition Grants   7,036,000
    Indian Student Grants   1,100,000
        All programs   21,048,000

Wyoming
    Student Incentive Grant Program   56,000

American Samoa
    Scholarship Program   293,000

Guam
    Professional/Technical Awards   231,000

Puerto Rico
    Incentive Grants   1,092,000

Trust Territory
    Scholarships and Grants   560,000

Virgin Islands
    Territorial Scholarships   487,000

6

Let Someone Else Help You Find
Your Scholarship

Millions of dollars worth of scholarships, grants and other financial aid go unclaimed every year. Last year alone, $135 million
was not claimed. These funds go unused because people do not
know where to look for scholarships.

Parents and students often depend on the schools to help
them find scholarship funds. The fact is that teachers, guidance
counselors and financial aid officers lack both the time and the
comprehensive knowledge that would enable them to provide
a complete listing of sources.

So resourceful students should investigate possibilities on
their own. Never assume that you are not eligible for scholarships; there might very well be a good scholarship for you if
you start to look early.

Use the Data Bank of The Scholarship Search.

One of the best resources for discovering available scholarship
money is The Scholarship Search Company which maintains the
largest scholarship information data bank in the United States.
The more than 250,000 scholarships listed are worth over $500
million.

The student's first step is to request an application from The
Scholarship Search, 1775 Broadway, New York, NY 10019. Your
detailed answers on the question application form you receive
will help the computer match your qualifications to the specifica-
tions of the 250,000 scholarships. This service will cost you $45.

51

The following sampling from The Scholarship Search will give you an idea of the awards you might qualify for.

Methodist National Scholarship
One-year nonrenewable scholarship; value $500; number varies
Based on religion
  Department of Student Scholarships
  Board of Education of Methodist Church
  P.O. Box 871
  Nashville, TN 38102

General Kosciuszko Grant-in-Aid
Based on ethnic background
  Value $1,000; number varies
  Kosciuszko Foundation
  15 East 65th Street
  New York, NY 10021

Gannett Newspaper Carrier Award
Four-year scholarship; value $4,000; number varies
  Frank Gannett Scholarships, Inc.
  49 South Fitzhugh Street
  Rochester, NY 14614

National Society of Professional Engineers Grants
One-year grant; value $1,000; number of awards: 30
Scholarship Chairman
  National Society of Professional Engineers
  2029 K Street, NW
  Washington, D.C. 20006

Engineering Scholarship
One-year renewable scholarship; value $1,000; number varies
Scholarship Committee
  Association of General Contractors Education Fund
  1957 E Street, NW
  Washington, D.C. 20006

Alcoa Foundation Scholarship
Four-year scholarship; value $4,000; number varies
Based on parents' employment
  Works Administration
  Alcoa Foundation

1501 Alcoa Building
Pittsburgh, PA 15219

Navy Relief Educational Fund
Value $100 to $1,250; number varies
Based on parents' military service
Navy Relief Society
N. Randolph Street
Arlington, VA 22203

E. C. Hallbeck Scholarship
Four-year award; value $2,000; number of awards: 10
Based on parents' union affiliation
Scholarship Committee
American Postal Workers Union
817 14th Street, NW
Washington, D.C. 20005

Association Scholarship
Value $500; number varies
Based on applicant's affiliation
Association of the Sons of Poland
665 Newark Avenue
Jersey City, NJ 07306

In most cases, students receive a computer report twelve to sixteen days after their applications reach The Scholarship Search. Ninety percent of all student applications are given at least five sources of money for college, according to the director. Most applicants have been put in touch with ten to fifteen sources of funds worth $10,000 to $15,000 per applicant, for which they qualified.

Other categories of awards in The Scholarship Search's data bank may surprise you. Harvard University gives scholarships to students whose names are Anderson, Broden, Downer, Haven and Murphy, among others.

At Yale University, if your name is Leavenworth or DeForest, they will grant you a $1,000 scholarship. There are awards for golf caddies, newspaper carriers, cheerleaders, glee clubbers, band players and students with handicaps. Among all these various opportunities, surely you are likely to strike gold!

Numerous Scholarships Are Awarded in Contests

Many scholarships are not claimed because they require applicants to write an essay or enter a contest. Students are generally reluctant to do this, though the possible reward is well worth the effort.

The American Legion for years has been sponsoring nationwide essay contests whose winners receive valuable scholarships.

To provide information about the various state legion scholarships, the national organization for twenty-eight years has printed an annual booklet, "Need a Lift?" To obtain it, send fifty cents to the American Legion, Emblem Sales Department, P.O. Box 1055, Indianapolis, IN 46206.

The deadline for most American Legion scholarships is March 15; their monetary values often vary, depending on local units, success in obtaining funds, but some awards are clearly defined, as we will note in the examples that follow.

National American Legion Auxiliary Presidents' Scholarships
Five scholarships of $1,500, 5 of $1,000; no field of specialization. Based on parents being veterans of World War I, World War II, Korean or Vietnam war

Department Secretary
American Legion Auxiliary
371 Morris Ave.
Elizabeth, NJ 07208

American Legion National High School Oratorical Contest
Scholarship value: winner, $8,000; runner-up, $5,000; third place, $3,000; fourth place, $2,000. Each state winner receives $500. Additional scholarships are awarded at the local and district levels. Based on public speaking and forensic ability in a prepared oration plus an extemporaneous discussion. Contestants do not have to be children of veterans. Contact the American Legion adjutant at local American Legion post

Eight and Forty Lung and Respiratory Nursing Scholarships
(The Eight and Forty chapter is the special fraternal organization of the American Legion Auxiliary.) Value $1,500; awarded to nursing students who expect to work full time in lung and respiratory medicine

American Legion Education and Scholarship Program
Eight and Forty Scholarships
P.O. Box 1055
Indianapolis, IN 46206

American Legion Auxiliary Scholarship at Alabama Colleges

Value $200; 20 scholarships granted. Recipients must reside in Alabama and be blood relatives of World War I or II veterans. Deadline May 1. Contact American Legion Auxiliary President at local American Legion Post in Alabama

Wilma D. Hoyal Memorial Scholarship

For political science majors at Arizona state colleges. Value $200; renewable for full-time students

Executive Secretary
American Legion Auxiliary
601 West Mission Lane
Phoenix, AZ 85021

California Auxiliary Americanism Essay Contest

Based on merit of writing in state essay contest, value $1,000.

American Legion Auxiliary Headquarters
113 War Memorial Building
San Francisco, CA 94102

California Legion Auxiliary Gift Scholarships

Value $800, $200 a year for 4 years; number of awards: 5. Based on parents being veterans of World War I, World War II, Korean or Vietnam wars; 5 years' residence in California required.

American Legion Auxiliary Headquarters
113 War Memorial Building
San Francisco, CA 94102

Connecticut Auxiliary Memorial Scholarships

Value $400; number of awards: 5, of which one is for nursing based on parents being veterans; Connecticut residence required

Department Auxiliary Headquarters
State Office Building
Hartford, CT 06115

Illinois Auxiliary Vocational and Business Scholarships

Value $400. Based on recipients' studying for vocational and business career; must be children of veterans and residents of Illinois.

Illinois Auxiliary Gift Scholarships

Value $1,000 and $600

American Legion Auxiliary
35 East Wacker Drive
Chicago, IL 60601

Mary Virginia Macrea Memorial Nurses' Scholarships
> Value $400. Based on applicants being mother, daughter, sister, wife or widow of a veteran of World War I or II or Korean war, and an Iowa resident. Note: This auxiliary also awards thirteen $300 scholarships to members of Legion and Auxiliary, and children of veterans of World War I or II and Korean war.
>> Department Executive Secretary
>> American Legion Auxiliary
>> 720 Lyon
>> Des Moines, IA 50316

Massachusetts Auxiliary Gift Scholarships
> Value 1 at $500, 10 at $100. Based on being children of deceased veterans and residents of Massachusetts.
>> Department Secretary
>> American Legion Auxiliary
>> 546-2 State House
>> Boston, MA 02133

American Legion Auxiliary Memorial Scholarships
> Michigan. Value $500. Applicants must be daughters of honorably discharged or deceased men and women veterans and residents of Michigan. Note: This auxiliary awards the Past President's Parley Scholarships of $500 each for one year's training for registered or practical nurses.
>> American Legion Auxiliary
>> 212 North Verlinden Street
>> Lansing, MI 48915

Florence O'Neill Scholarships
> Value $250; number of awards: 4. For residents of Minnesota attending school in Minnesota.

Blanche Wallace Scallen Scholarship
> Value $250. For child of veteran entering the field of vocational training in education and in teaching the mentally retarded.
>> Department Headquarters
>> American Legion Auxiliary
>> State Veterans Service Building
>> Columbus Drive
>> St. Paul, MN 55155

Nurse Gift Tuition Scholarships
> Value $200; number as permitted by funds available

Practical Nurse Scholarships
Value $100. For children of veterans who are Nebraska residents in financial need

Forgotten Children Scholarships
Value $200. For students who are not children of veterans; five-year residence in Nebraska required.

Averyl Elaine Keriakedes Memorial Scholarship
Value $450. For a woman student, related to a veteran, who plans to become a teacher.
>Department Secretary
>American Legion Auxiliary
>P.O. Box 5227, Station C
>Lincoln, NE 65805

Grace S. High Memorial Child Welfare Scholarships
Value $200; number of awards: 2. For daughters of legionnaires or auxiliary members.

Elsie B. Brown Scholarships
Value $150. For daughters of deceased veterans attending any school of higher learning in New Hampshire.
>Department Secretary
>American Legion Auxiliary
>407 State House Annex
>Concord, NH 03301

Nursing Scholarships
Value $1,000; number of awards: 10, one in each Judicial District of New York State. Awarded to daughters of living or deceased veterans, under 20 years of age; must show financial need and be New York State residents.
>Department Secretary
>American Legion Auxiliary
>346 Broadway, Room 816
>New York, NY 10013

Past President's Parley Scholarships
Value $100; number of awards: 4. For use in nurses' training for daughter of legionnaire or member of auxiliary who resides in North Dakota. Also, if funds permit, 5 scholarships, value $100, for residents of North Dakota already attending a university or state college.

Department Secretary
American Legion Auxiliary
1806 7th Avenue, N. W.
Minot, ND 58701

Past President's Parley Nursing Scholarships

Value $300; awarded to as many women as auxiliary has funds. For daughters
of World War I or II or Korean or Vietnam war veterans; must be Ohio residents. Also, one $1,000 scholarship for daughter of World War I or II or
Korean or Vietnam war veteran; Ohio residency required.

Department Secretary
American Legion Auxiliary
737 Forest Avenue
Zanesville, OH 43701

Nurses Training Scholarships

Value $1,500; for 3 years. Awarded to sons or daughters of veterans, ac-
cepted by a hospital or university school of nursing in Oregon; must be
Oregon resident. Also, $500 grants, one-time, for sons, daughters, widows
of veterans or wives of disabled veterans, residents in Oregon; must be
used in an accredited school in Oregon. Also, one scholarship for veteran,
child of veteran or widow of veteran; must be used in accredited school in
Oregon, in field of children and youth.

Chairman, Education and Scholarships
American Legion Auxiliary
421 S.W. Fifth Avenue
Portland, OR 97204

Pennsylvania Scholarship

Value $750; number of awards: 1. For daughters of veterans in need of
financial aid; must be Pennsylvania residents.

Nurse's Training

Value $600; number awarded: 1. Renewable for four years. For daughter
of a deceased or totally disabled veteran.

Past President's Parley

Value $600; number awarded: 1. For daughter of a living veteran.

Department Chairman, Education and Scholarships
American Legion Auxiliary
P.O. Box 2643
Harrisburg, PA 17105

Rhode Island Scholarship

Value $250; number awarded: 1. For the daughter of an honorably discharged veteran: must attend any accredited Rhode Island school; must show financial need.

American Legion Auxiliary
c/o Rhode Island Legion
Veterans Memorial Building, Room 408
Providence, RI 02903

Gift Scholarships to Junior Members

Value $250; number awarded: 2. For South Carolina junior members with a consecutive 3-year membership at time of application.

Gift Scholarships to Girls State Participants

Value $100; number awarded: 2. For girls who attended Girls State the previous year.

Department Secretary
American Legion Auxiliary
132 Picken Street
Columbia, SC 29205

Nurses' Scholarship

Value $200; number awarded: 3. For sons and daughters of veterans or auxiliary members; must be residents of South Dakota.

Vocational Scholarship

Value $150; number awarded: 1. For son or daughter of veteran or auxiliary member.

Gift Scholarship

Value $300; number awarded: 2. For sons and daughters of any veterans, resident in South Dakota.

Department Secretary
American Legion Auxiliary
Bruce, SD 57720

Nursing Scholarships

Value $150 number awarded: 6. For child or other dependent of veteran; resident of Tennesee.

Gift Scholarships

Value $150; number awarded: 6. For child or other dependent of veteran; resident of Tennessee.

Department Headquarters
American Legion Auxiliary
1922 Broad Street
Nashville, TN 37203

Nurses' Scholarships
Value $300. For children of veterans; residents of Texas.

General Education Scholarships
Value $300. For children of veterans; residents of Texas.
Department Headquarters
American Legion Auxiliary
709 East 10th Street
Austin, TX 78701

Good Citizenship Awards
Four one-year tuition scholarships. Given for good citizenship to women attending Utah Girls' State.
American Legion Auxiliary
B-25 State Capitol Building
Salt Lake City, UT 84114

Susan Burdett Scholarship
Value $200. For a Girls' State student of previous year.

Schwarz Vocational Scholarship
For a veteran's child; must be resident of Washington.

Nurses' Scholarship
Value $200. For a veteran's child; must be resident of Washington.
American Legion Auxiliary
414 Olive Way
Seattle, WA 98101

Department Presidents' Special Scholarship Project
Value $500; number awarded: 6. For daughters, granddaughters, wives or widows of deceased or disabled veterans attending a college or university in Wisconsin. Value $500; number awarded: 5. For daughters or granddaughters of veterans.

Macauley, Eleanor Smith and Harriett Hass Awards
Value $500; number awarded: 3. For daughters or granddaughters of veterans living or dead.

Department Scholarships

Value $500; number awarded: 5. For daughters of veterans planning on taking registered nurse training. Value $550; number awarded: 3. For a teacher of history or social science.

Department Executive Secretary
American Legion Auxiliary
812 East State Street
Milwaukee, WI 53202

7

Basic Educational Opportunity Grants

President Carter and Congress are trying to help families of college students, especially the middle-income family, to meet the costs of attending college.

In November 1978 the president signed a new law that improves the Basic Educational Opportunity Grant program. Beginning with the 1979–1980 academic year, students from families making as much as $26,000 annually may qualify for grants of $200 or more. Everyone in the middle-income group should now apply for these funds that formerly were available only to lower-income families.

The Basic Educational Opportunity Grant Program

"Basic" describes the program very well, for the funds available are meant to pay basic expenses of a student's education. The Basic Opportunity Grant will seldom cover all college expenses; it is the *base* on which other financial aid awards are built. Students who receive these funds usually need additional money to attend college.

Financial need is the key to getting financial aid under the Basic Educational Opportunity program. The federal government has established its own system to determine a family's financial need. This formula is approved each year by Congress, and as a result the methods for judging your family's financial need will change each year, as will the amount of aid available to you, which depends on the dollars Congress allocates each year.

Who Is Eligible for the Basic Grants?

To be eligible for the Basic Educational Grants you must:

1. Be a citizen or a permanent resident of the United States.

2. Be enrolled at least half time as a student at an eligible college—that is, one accredited by the U.S. Office of Education.

3. Have financial need as determined by the U.S. Office of Education. This is important: no one at your college will be able to judge your financial need for this program. Only the federal government has this authority.

Obviously, students will be eligible for this grant, provided that they can demonstrate financial need.

How Do I Apply for This Program?

We suggest that you make application early in January. This will allow you to know the amount of grant you may receive from the program so that you can plan further. Also, you will then have all the documents you need from the federal government by the time you reach college in September. Without those documents you may not be able to register for college, unless you or your family has the cash.*

You may use one of four methods to apply for a Basic Educational Opportunity Grant.

1. The Financial Aid Form distributed by the College Scholarship Service. Block No. 83 on page 11 of this form states that if you check "yes," information may be released for this program. You may also name two colleges to which the Basic Educational Opportunity Grant program will provide your own Basic Grant status.

2. The Family Financial Statement, distributed by the American College Testing Program, which has the same general format as the Financial Aid Form.

3. The Federal Basic Educational Opportunity Grant Program application. After completion, this is mailed by the student

* Note: You cannot get a grant for more than four years—or five years in the case of certain special five-year courses.

directly to the Basic Grant Program, P.O. Box A, Iowa City, IA 52240.

4. The Pennsylvania Higher Education Assistance Agency Application, for Pennsylvania residents only, which has the same basic format as the FAF and FFS, above.

Both the College Scholarship Service and the American College Testing Program documents are generally used to apply not only for Basic Grants, but for state and college financial aid programs. You should use either of these documents if you intend to apply for funds in addition to the Basic Grant. (The Pennsylvania Higher Education Assistance Agency form is used to apply for state financial aid programs as well as the Basic Grant.)

The federal application form should be used only when you will apply for no other aid but the Basic Educational Opportunity Grant.

How Much Money Might Be Available to the Student?

For the 1978–1979 academic year, you might have received from $200 to $1,600, depending on your financial need as calculated by the U.S. Office of Education. You can determine exactly how much money you may receive only by taking the student eligibility report to a college you wish to attend. You will receive the eligibility report direct from the federal government, six to eight weeks after filing one of the applications described above.

A student eligibility report contains four sections.

Section I is a summary of the information you and your family reported on your application for the Basic Grant. You should check it carefully; if there are errors, you *must* report them by removing the last page of the document, drawing a line through the incorrect information, writing the correct data above that line, signing the certification on back of the form (both student and parent) and sending it to the Basic Educational Opportunity Program, P.O. Box C, Iowa City, IA 52240. You will then receive a corrected document.

Section II contains comments on your application and your

student eligibility index number. The financial aid director will use this number to calculate the amount of your Basic Grant. Generally, the lower the number, the higher your award will be.

Section III contains an *estimate* of your Basic Grant award, assuming that you are a full-time student. Be cautious in accepting this estimate; it will take a financial aid officer to translate it into the award that you will receive at your college.

Section IV will be completed by the school in which you enroll and will eventually result in payment to the school of your Basic Grant funds.

If you are unable to take the student eligibility report personally to the financial aid office at the college that you will attend, mail the document by certified mail, return receipt requested, to the financial aid office at the college. The financial aid officer will then compute the exact amount of your Basic Grant award and inform you.

The amount of the Basic Grant may well vary with the cost of the college. Generally, the higher the college costs, the higher the grant.

The following examples show the specific dollar amounts that different families would receive in Basic Grants at different colleges. Each family has net assets of less than $17,000 and consists of two parents and one dependent child who will be attending college full time.

Example 1. Family with an Income After Taxes of $6,000.

The net assets of this family are below $25,000.

Anna Green has applied to seven colleges and been accepted by all of them. She also applied for and received a Basic Grant.

The actual amount of money she gets from the Basic Grant will depend on which college she chooses.

Regardless of the cost of the college she attends, Anna cannot receive more than $1,444 as her Basic Grant. This is the maximum amount she can receive; it is determined by her family income and assets.

At Yale, she would undoubtedly qualify for considerable additional financial aid from the university. At Florida A & M, the

College	Estimated Cost	Approximate Basic Grant Award
Florida A & M (commuter)	$1,800	$ 912
Abraham Baldwin (Georgia)	2,200	1,112
Western Illinois	3,500	1,762
Michigan State	4,300	1,800
UCLA	5,600	1,800
Yale	8,000	1,800
Northern Florida Community College (commuter)	1,600	812

amount Anna would need over and above her Basic Grant would be much less than at Yale.

Obviously, her Basic Grant would not be enough to pay all of her college costs at any of these institutions.

Anna had decided to attend Florida A & M, and she will visit the financial aid director there to plan for the extra money she will need to attend the college.

Example 2. Family with an Income After Taxes of $8,000.

John Brown has applied to the same colleges as Anna Green. However, his Basic Grant will be less than Anna's because his

College	Estimated Cost	Approximate Basic Grant Award
Florida A & M (commuter)	$1,800	$ 912
Abraham Baldwin (Georgia)	2,200	1,112
Western Illinois	3,500	1,676
Michigan State	4,300	1,676
UCLA	5,600	1,676
Yale	8,000	1,676
Northern Florida Community College (commuter)	1,600	812

family had $2,000 more income than her family had.

His discussions with the financial aid directors indicated the Basic Grant money that he would receive at each of the colleges.

John's maximum Basic Grant will be $1,090 no matter what college he attends.

As with Anna Green, his choice of college to attend will depend on what financial aid he might receive in addition to the Basic Grant award.

Example 3. Family with an Income After Taxes of $10,000.

Jean Gray applied to the same colleges as Anna Green and John Brown. But the income of the Gray family was $2,000 more than that of the Brown family, and Jean's Basic Grant award was smaller.

College	Estimated Cost	Approximate Basic Grant Award
Florida A & M (commuter)	$1,800	$ 912
Abraham Baldwin (Georgia)	2,200	1,112
Western Illinois	3,500	1,476
Michigan State	4,300	1,476
UCLA	5,600	1,476
Yale	8,000	1,476
Northern Florida Community College (commuter)	1,600	812

The most Jean can expect from a Basic Grant, regardless of the cost of the individual college, is $802. The higher the cost of attendance, the more she must depend on additional financial aid directly from the college, or on money her parents can afford to pay toward her tuition, room and board.

Example 4. Family with an Income After Taxes of $20,000.

James Smith was in the same class with Anna Green, John Brown and Jean Gray and decided to apply to the same colleges.

Note the effect of the higher income of the Smith family—

College	Estimated Cost	Approximate Basic Grant Award
Florida A & M (commuter)	$1,800	$676
Abraham Baldwin (Georgia)	2,200	676
Western Illinois	3,500	676
Michigan State	4,300	676
UCLA	5,600	676
Yale	8,000	676
Northern Florida Community College (commuter)	1,600	500

an increase of $10,000 over the Gray family income.

If James attends Northern Florida Community College, he will receive no Basic Grant at all. Elsewhere, his maximum Basic Grant would be $676. He would have to go to the financial aid directors at these colleges to get more information about the other kinds of financial aid he could obtain.

As of this writing, it is unlikely that a dependent student (from a family with two parents and one dependent child) whose family's income exceeded $25,000 would receive any Basic Grant at all.

Supplementary Educational Opportunity Grants

The Supplementary Educational Opportunity Grant is a gift of funds to a student; the student does not have to work for it or repay it.

To qualify for this program a student must have *exceptional* financial need. This means that the amount that parents can be expected to contribute must be less than one half of the college cost of tuition, room, board and miscellaneous expenses.

For example, if you are accepted at a college where you have to pay $4,000, you can receive a SEOG if your parents are able to contribute *less than* $2,000.

What Are the Qualifications for Obtaining a SEOG?

1. You must be a citizen or a permanent resident of the United States. Those who have only a student visa are ineligible for this program.

2. A student must exhibit financial need. The financial aid officer will decide what students are eligible for the grant.

3. A student must be accepted for enrollment or be enrolled at least half time at an eligible college.

4. If you are attending college at the direction of a church or a religious order, you are not eligible.

5. A student who is in default in any federal loan program or who owes the college money is not eligible.

6. A student must demonstrate to the college evidence of academic or creative promise and the capability to maintain good standing in the courses he or she has chosen.

7. All SEOG participants must be undergraduates. This means that you must not have received a B.A. degree.

A student may receive these grants for four years, or for five years if enrolled in a five-year program. If the college determines that you are in need of an additional year of study, an exception can be made.

While the college determines the specific amount of the grant you will receive, the maximum award is $1,500 per year and the minimum is $200.

8

Guaranteed Student Loans

The one federally supported program for middle-income groups is the state or federal Guaranteed Student Loan Program. Generally you can borrow up to $7,500 for four undergraduate years. Funds are available from local financial institutions, and there are no repayment responsibilities while student status exists and for nine months thereafter. A loan is made to the student, not to the parents; the student, not the parents, is obligated to repay.

You don't have to begin to repay a loan until nine months after you cease to be a student. Then federal law requires a minimum monthly payment of $30, the total to be paid back within a maximum term of ten years.

Many students fail to realize that they can pay much of their own college costs, perhaps all of them at a state university, with the help of a guaranteed loan.

When you consider the actual costs of attending college, don't underestimate the price of books and other miscellaneous expenses. These costs can run as high as $700 at a state university; books alone can cost at least $200 per semester.

A very lean estimate of personal expenses over the academic year, including laundry and entertainment, would be $20 per week. It is in this area that most students overspend—especially those students who have not been away from home before. Students who have had little experience in budgeting their money may run into serious financial problems.

Parents who do not begin the budget lessons and lectures long before the student leaves for college may be the recipients

of many "send money quickly" telephone calls.

In the area of transportation, the estimated expense will be determined by the cost of round-trip fares and how often the student may be coming home. One must also allow for trips to be taken in emergencies or to attend family social gatherings.

If we add the real costs of an education to the budgets we have discussed, the total cost for four years might be much higher than the $32,000 we mentioned.

How to Apply for a Guaranteed Student Loan

Many students and parents do not know they are eligible for a Guaranteed Student Loan. This is especially true of middle-income families. In fact, any student, no matter what his or her family income, is eligible for a loan; no student is disqualified because of family income.

However, it is important to remember that banks participating in the Guaranteed Student Loan Program do not have to lend students money. The decision is a purely banking decision; it is, after all, the bank's money. All the government does is guarantee the payment to the bank of the principal (if students do not repay it) and sometimes the interest.

So the first principle in applying for the loan is: Be nice.

These are the procedures for applying for a Guaranteed Student Loan:

1. You must be accepted in an accredited educational institution (a vocational, college, university, or other post-secondary institution).

2. Go to a financial institution such as a bank or a savings and loan association. A bank or savings and loan association that you or your parents do business with will be more inclined to help you. If this bank cannot give you a loan, you will have to shop other banks. If your bank does not grant GSL loans, perhaps the officers can tell you of a bank that does.

3. Ask for a GSL application. The bank will have application blanks if they are making these loans. The application contains sections to be filled out by the students, the parents and the school.

4. Parents and student fill out their sections of the application form and forward it to the college. The college should be asked to return the application blank to the family, *not* to the bank; this will insure that you know the status of the application.

5. When you receive the completed form from the college, take it to the bank.

6. After the bank receives the application blank, it will ask for government approval to process the form.

7. The bank will notify you when the approved loan is available. This should take at least six weeks. If you are a student intending to enroll in college in September, don't wait until June to apply for your loan. At that time you will be competing with so many other students that you might not receive your check in time for the September session.

8. The bank will ask you to pay for insurance coverage based on the amount of the loan. This can amount to $20 to $60.

9. After the insurance has been paid and the bank has secured approval from the federal government, a check will be drawn for the amount of the loan—and is usually made payable to both the student and the school.

How Do I Repay the Loan?

Your loan agreement requires that you contact the lender (your bank) when you leave school, reporting your change in status. Your bank will then discuss repayment terms with you and establish a repayment note.

Federal law requires a minimum monthly payment of $30 and a maximum term of ten years. Divide the total amount of the loan by 120, the maximum number of monthly payments, to find the amount of your monthly principal payments. Then add 7 percent interest to this amount, and you will have a close approximation of your monthly payment.

Suppose, for example, you owe $6,000. This amount divided by 120 gives you $50 per month repayment of principal. One year's interest on $6,000 at 7 percent is $420. Thus you pay $35 monthly in interest. Your total payment is $85 a month.

These loans are not grants; the federal or state government

must pay the bank if you fail to discharge your repayment responsibility.

A student who cannot make the payments should keep in touch with the lender and obtain *forbearance* (skipped payments or reduced payments) as provided by law.

You Don't Have to Work Your Way Through College If You Are Willing to Borrow.

The Guaranteed Student Loan Program is a boon to the middle-income family and will be in great demand. Students from families with incomes of $10,000 to $100,000 or more may borrow from their local bank, interest-free, as long as student status continues.

Since an undergraduate can borrow $7,500 over four years and a graduate student can borrow up to $15,000, this program can help you to borrow your way through college.

Because this loan is interest-free while you maintain student status, you may find it difficult to find banks willing to lend to you. Many are swamped with loan applications.

If you have trouble finding a bank with loans available, consult the listing of Guaranteed Student Loan Program offices that follows which can tell you where to locate a bank that will lend to you.

Alabama
  Regional Administrator
  Office of Education, Regional IV
  50 Seventh Street, N.E.
  Atlanta, GA 30323

Alaska
  Student Aid Office
  State Education Department
  Pouch F, AOB
  Juneau, AK 99801

Arizona
  Regional Administrator
  Office of Education, Regional IX
  50 United Nations Plaza
  San Francisco, CA 94102

Arkansas
Student Loan Guarantee Foundation of Arkansas
1515 West 7th Street, Suite 515
Little Rock, AR 72202

California
Regional Administrator
Office of Education, Region IX
50 United Nations Plaza
San Francisco, CA 94102

Colorado
Regional Administrator
Office of Education, Region VIII
11037 Federal Office Building
19th and Stout Streets
Denver, CO 80202

Connecticut
Connecticut Student Loan Foundation
25 Pratt Street
Hartford, CT 06103

Delaware
Delaware Higher Education Loan Program
c/o Brandywine College
P.O. Box 7139
Wilmington, DE 19803

District of Columbia
D.C. Student Loan Insurance Program
1329 E Street, N.W.
Washington, D.C. 20004

Florida
Florida Student Financial Assistance Commission
Knott Building, Room 563
Tallahassee, FL 32304

Georgia
Georgia Higher Education Assistance Corporation
9 LaVista Perimeter Park
2187 Northlake Parkway
Tucker, GA 30084

Hawaii

Regional Administrator
Office of Education, Region IX
50 United Nations Plaza
San Francisco, CA 94102

Idaho

Regional Administrator
Office of Education, Region X
1321 Second Avenue
Seattle, WA 98101

Illinois

Illinois Guaranteed Loan Program
102 Wilmot Road
Deerfield, IL 60015

Indiana

State Student Assistance Commission
219 N. Seante Avenue, Second Floor
Indianapolis, IN 46202

Iowa

Regional Administrator
Office of Education, Region VII
601 East 12th Street
Kansas City, MO 64106

Kansas

Higher Education Assistance Foundation
51 Corporate Woods
9393 West 110th Street, Suite 405
Overland Park, KS 66210

Louisiana

Louisiana Higher Education Assistance Commission
P.O. Box 44127
Capitol Station
Baton Rouge, LA 70804

Maine

Maine State Department of Education and Cultural Services
Augusta, ME 04330

Maryland
> Maryland Higher Education Loan Corporation
> 2100 Guilford Avenue
> Baltimore, MD 21218

Massachusetts
> Massachusetts Higher Education Assistance Corporation
> 1010 Park Square Building
> Boston, MA 02116

Michigan
> Michigan Higher Education Assistance Authority
> 309 N. Washington Avenue
> Lansing, MI 48902

Minnesota
> Higher Education Assistance Foundation
> 1100 Northwestern Bank Building
> 55 East 5th Street
> St. Paul, MN 55101

Mississippi
> Regional Administrator
> Office of Education, Region VII
> 50 Seventh Street, N.E.
> Atlanta, GA 30323

Missouri
> Regional Administrator
> Office of Education, Region VII
> 601 East 12th Street
> Kansas City, MO 64106

Montana
> Regional Administrator
> Office of Education, Region VIII
> 11037 Federal Office Building
> 19th and Stout Streets
> Denver, CO 80202

Nebraska
> Regional Administrator
> Office of Education, Region VII
> 601 East 12th Street
> Kansas City, MO 64106

Nevada
State Department of Education
Carson City, NV 89701

New Hampshire
New Hampshire Higher Education Assistance Foundation
143 North Main Street
Concord, NH 03301

New Jersey
New Jersey Higher Education Assistance Authority
1474 Prospect Street
P.O. Box 1417
Trenton, NJ 08625

New Mexico
Regional Administrator
Office of Education, Region VI
1200 Main Tower Building, 15th Floor
Dallas, TX 75202

New York
New York State Higher Education Services Corporation
Tower Building
Empire State Plaza
Albany, NY 12255

North Carolina
North Carolina State Education Assistance Authority
P.O. Box 2688
Chapel Hill, NC 27514

North Dakota
Regional Administrator
Office of Education, Region VIII
11037 Federal Office Building
19th and Stout Streets
Denver, CO 80202

Ohio
Ohio Student Loan Commission
34 North High Street
Columbus, OH 43215

Oklahoma
>Oklahoma State Regents for Higher Education
>500 Education Building
>State Capitol Complex
>Oklahoma City, OK 73105

Oregon
>State of Oregon Scholarship Commission
>1445 Willamette Street
>Eugene, OR 97401

Pennsylvania
>Pennsylvania Higher Education Assistance Agency
>Towne House
>660 Boas Street
>Harrisburg, PA 17102

Puerto Rico
>Regional Administrator
>Office of Education, Region II
>26 Federal Plaza
>New York, NY 10022

Rhode Island
>Rhode Island Higher Education Assistance Corporation
>187 Westminster Mall
>Room 414, Box 579
>Providence, RI 02901

South Carolina
>Regional Administrator
>Office of Education, Region IV
>50 Seventh Street, N.E.
>Atlanta, GA 30323

South Dakota
>Regional Administrator
>Office of Education, Region VIII
>11037 Federal Office Building
>19th and Stout Streets
>Denver, CO 80202

Tennessee
Tennessee Student Assistance Corporation
707 Main Street
Nashville, TN 37206

Texas
Regional Administrator
Office of Education, Region VI
1200 Main Tower Building, 15th Floor
Dallas, TX 75201

Utah
Utah Higher Education Assistance Authority
807 East South Temple, Suite 301
Salt Lake City, UT 84103

Vermont
Vermont Student Assistance Corporation
156 College Street
Burlington, VT 05401

Virginia
Virginia State Educational Assistance Authority
501 East Franklin Street
Suite 311, Professional Building
Richmond, VA 23219

Washington
Regional Administrator
Office of Education, Region C
1321 Second Avenue
Seattle, WA 98101

West Virginia
Regional Administrator
Office of Education, Region III
P.O. Box 13716
3535 Market Street
Philadelphia, PA 19101

Wisconsin
Wisconsin Higher Education Corporation
123 West Washington Avenue
Madison, WI 53703

Wyoming
Regional Administrator
Office of Education, Region VIII
11037 Federal Office Building
19th and Stout Streets
Denver, CO 80202

A Selection of Other Loan Programs

Medical Education Loan Guarantee Program

The American Medical Association Education and Research Foundation has established a Medical Education Loan Guarantee Program to help qualified students with financial need who are enrolled in an approved training institution.

The loan program is extended to medical students, interns and residents. For information about this program, consult the financial aid officer at your medical school or write The American Medical Association Education and Research Foundation, 535 N. Dearborn, Chicago, IL 60610.

The American Fund for Mental Health

The American Fund for Dental Health provides a guaranteed loan program for undergraduate and graduate students to help meet financial need. The program is intended to *supplement* other loan programs or opportunities.

Any dental student who is a U.S. citizen is eligible to apply. The maximum loan obtainable for an academic year is $5,000; the total amount one student may borrow is $17,500. Applications are available only from the dental school's financial aid officer.

The United Student Aid Funds

The United Student Aid Funds programs offer loans of $2,500 yearly to a maximum of $7,500 for undergraduates and loans of up to $15,000 for graduate students. The loans carry a 7 percent simple interest rate.

Loans to professional students in the fields of medicine, dentistry and osteopathy (up to $5,000 yearly, to a maximum of $17,500, with an anticipated simple interest rate of approximately 10 percent) are made by selected participating lending institutions and guaranteed by United Student Aid Funds under a program sponsored by the Robert Wood Johnson Foundation.

For further information, write United Student Aid Funds, Inc., 6610 North Shadeland Avenue, P.O. Box 50827, Indianapolis, IN 46250.

The loan funds administered by United Student Aid Funds are private; in other respects, this program is very similar to the federal Guaranteed Student Loan Program.

Indian Tribal Grants and Loans

Indian Tribal Grants and Loans have been established by more than forty-five Indian tribes to promote higher education for their members. Applications for assistance should be made through the U.S. Department of the Interior, Bureau of Indian Affairs, Washington, D.C. 20242.

The Bill Cosby-Crest Student Loan Fund

The Bill Cosby-Crest Student Loan Fund is a source of financial assistance for dental students whose family incomes are less than $15,000 annually. Loans range from $2,500 to $3,333 per year, up to a total of $10,000 for any one student.

Applications may be obtained from the financial aid officer at the student's dental school.

The American Optometric Association has provided funds to establish a special reserve with the United Student Aid Funds, enabling optometry students to borrow from financial institutions at a low interest rate. United Student Aid Funds guarantees the loan, with the support of the AOA reserve.

To qualify for the loan, the AOA student must be in good academic standing and pursuing a Doctor of Optometry degree. He or she must also demonstrate financial need.

An eligible student may borrow up to $5,000 per academic

year and up to $15,000 for an entire academic career, including undergraduate and graduate study. For information, write American Optometric Association, 243 North Lindbergh Boulevard, St. Louis, MO 63141.

9

Obtaining a National Direct Student Loan

The National Direct Student loan is a loan from the federal government that is paid directly to the university. It carries a low interest rate (3 percent) and a long repayment term (ten years).

Who Is Eligible?

The following criteria must be met in order to be eligible for a National Direct Student loan.

1. A student must exhibit financial need. The financial aid officer decides which students are eligible for this loan.

2. A student must be a citizen or a permanent resident of the United States. Those who have only a student visa are ineligible for this program.

3. A student must be accepted for enrollment or be enrolled at least half time at a qualifying college.

4. A student who is attending college at the direction of a church or religious order is not eligible.

5. A student must indicate that he or she is willing to repay the loan.

6. A student who is in default in any federal loan program, or who owes the college money, may not be eligible.

Loans may be paid to the student borrower by the institution. However, the proceeds of the loan are usually credited to the student's account at the university, and the university then charges the account for tuition, room and board.

How Much May the Student Borrow?

1. You can borrow up to $2,500 during your first two years in college.

2. When you have completed two years, you can borrow up to $5,000 (including what you have already borrowed).

3. If you are a junior or a senior in college, you may borrow $2,500 for each of these two years.

4. Graduate or professional students may borrow up to $10,000. (If you have already borrowed $5,000 as an undergraduate, you may borrow only $5,000 more.)

These loans remain interest-free while a student continues to study at least half time. If you leave college, or if your status falls below that of a half-time student, you have nine months more before interest begins on the loan. The interest is 3 percent per year (simple interest) on the outstanding balance.

What Are the Repayment Terms?

1. The loan is to be repaid monthly, bimonthly or quarterly, as desired by the college that loaned you the money.

2. Repayment begins nine months after the borrower's status as a student studying at least half time ends.

3. You have ten years to repay the loan.

4. Borrowers may repay all or any part of the loan at an earlier date.

5. The college usually requires a minimum payment of $30 monthly, $60 bimonthly or $120 per quarter.

6. Should the borrower fail to meet a scheduled payment of any installment, the college may declare the entire amount of the loan due and payable.

A student who has a problem meeting a scheduled payment should get in touch with the college business office. They will help you work out your payment so that you will not default on your loan.

It is a wise policy to report any personal change of address to the business office, so that the college can always get in touch with you if necessary.

Sample Repayment Schedule for a National Direct Student Loan

Monthly Payment Number	Amount Financed	Finance Charge*	Principal Payment	Total Payment
1	$1,000	$ 2.50	$ 30	$ 32.50
2	970	2.43	30	32.43
3	940	2.35	30	32.35
4	910	2.28	30	32.28
5	880	2.20	30	32.20
6	850	2.13	30	32.13
7	820	2.05	30	32.05
8	790	1.98	30	31.98
9	760	1.90	30	31.90
10	730	1.83	30	31.83
11	700	1.75	30	31.75
12	670	1.68	30	31.68
13	640	1.60	30	31.60
14	610	1.53	30	31.53
15	580	1.45	30	31.45
16	550	1.38	30	31.38
17	520	1.30	30	31.30
18	490	1.23	30	31.23
19	460	1.15	30	31.15
20	430	1.08	30	31.08
21	400	1.00	30	31.00
22	370	.93	30	30.93
23	340	.85	30	30.85
24	310	.78	30	30.78
25	280	.70	30	30.70
26	250	.63	30	30.63
27	220	.55	30	30.55
28	190	.48	30	30.48
29	160	.40	30	30.40
30	130	.33	30	30.33
31	100	.25	30	30.25
32	70	.18	30	30.18
33	40	.10	30	30.10
34	10	.03	10	10.03
TOTALS		$43.01	$1,000	$1,043.01

* The finance charge is computed at 3 percent per annum on the unpaid principal balance.

If a student transfers to another college, any outstanding loan must then be repaid. The only way to avoid immediate repayment is to have a deferment form signed by the registrar of the college to which you have transferred.

You will have to apply all over again, if you want to get a loan from the new college you attend.

To get a loan from your new college, you will have to get a deferment form signed and sent to the business office of the college you previously attended.

Can Loan Payments Be Canceled Under Special Circumstances?

There are certain circumstances which allow students to have their loan payments canceled.

1. *Teacher Cancellations.*

A borrower is entitled to have the entire amount of any loan plus the interest thereon canceled if he or she becomes a full-time teacher in a public or other nonprofit elementary or secondary school for handicapped children.

A borrower is entitled to have the entire amount of any loan plus the interest thereon canceled in return for services as a full-time teacher in a public or other nonprofit elementary or secondary school where there is a high concentration of students from low-income families. Consult the Federal Register for the names of designated schools, or ask your college business office.

The rates of cancellation for teachers in low-income schools and for teachers of the handicapped are: first year, 15 percent; second year, 15 percent; third year, 20 percent; fourth year, 20 percent; fifth year, 30 percent. At the end of five years, the entire loan has been canceled.

2. *Military Service Cancellation.*

A borrower is entitled to have up to 50 percent of any loan canceled if he or she is a member of the armed forces of the

United States in an area that qualifies for special pay. Further information will be available from your college business office.

3. *Death.*

Any loan may be canceled upon the death of the borrower.

4. *Permanent and Total Disability.*

Any loan may be canceled if the borrower becomes permanently and totally disabled.

5. *Head Start.*

A borrower may have the entire amount of a loan canceled for services as a full-time staff member in a preschool program carried out under Head Start.

The cancellation rate will be 15 percent per year, provided that the program is operated for a period comparable to a full school year. And the borrower's salary must not be more than the salary of a comparable employee of the local education agency.

6. *Bankruptcy.*

A loan shall be canceled upon the receipt of an official notice of discharge of bankruptcy from the bankruptcy court.

10

Paying for Your College Education
on the Installment Plan

No matter how hard you have been saving to pay for a college education, you may not have saved enough to meet the escalating cost of attending college.

If your middle-income family doesn't qualify for financial aid and your son or daughter announces he or she has been admitted to Harvard and needs $8,000 a year, don't panic! There are firms and colleges that will lend you money, and some plans will give you many years in which to repay.

The Parents' Loan Program involves loans to the parents, not to the student; it is the parents' responsibility to repay the loan.

The following examples are plans we've reviewed and found worthwhile and reasonable. These plans are available throughout the United States.

The Knight Agency Plan

The Knight Agency in Boston, Massachusetts, realizes the problem families face when they must meet large educational expenses, and it has come up with a repayment schedule that fits the individual's income.

Moreover, this plan includes an insurance policy, thereby assuring that students will not be forced to discontinue their education should the breadwinner become disabled or die.

The Knight Agency Plan is a low-cost insured loan. It permits parents with good credit reputations to spread the cost of college over long periods, according to their family income.

How Does the Plan Work?

1. The family decides how much it needs to borrow for the student's education; the members also determine their own ability to repay the loan.

2. The bank has to approve the family's credit.

When the credit has been approved, payment is made directly to the college in the amount agreed upon between the Knight Agency and the parents.

3. You can time the equal monthly repayments to correspond with the arrival of your paycheck, allowing you to set up your monthly budget in advance.

4. You can extend loan repayments over six years.

5. The insurance protection of the plan guarantees that if the breadwinner becomes disabled or dies, the student will not be forced to discontinue his or her education.

6. You determine the amount of money you need for college expenses each year. The amount you borrow can be adjusted up or down.

7. You can cancel the plan at any time upon written notice.

The following tables show the total costs of borrowing various amounts under the Knight Agency Plan. These monthly payments shown are approximate figures, based on a 1 percent per month finance charge and insurance on a parent between the ages of forty and fifty-five.

Four Years of College, 72 Monthly Payments

Annual Amount Borrowed	Monthly Payment	Total Cost
$1,000	$ 68	$ 4,797.01
2,000	135	9,630.85
3,000	202	14,462.61
4,000	269	19,294.41
5,000	336	24,126.22
6,000	403	28,957.95

Two Years of College, 36 Monthly Payments

Annual Amount Borrowed	Monthly Payment	Total Cost
$1,000	$ 64	$ 2,263.84
2,000	127	4,534.69
3,000	190	6,805.61
4,000	253	9,076.49
5,000	316	11,347.40
6,000	379	13,618.33

Girard Bank's Edu-Check Plan

The Girard Bank in Philadelphia, Pennsylvania, believes in helping parents "put their children through school painlessly." The bank has already helped 10,000 families to educate their children with Edu-Check.

Girard Bank provides money to pay all your student's education expenses after you have established a line of credit by signing an agreement with the bank to lend you the amount of money that you estimate you will need.

How Does the Plan Work?

1. You establish a line of credit to pay education expenses one year at a time, without renewing your agreement each year. You can provide for up to five years of education.

2. Girard Bank will send you a book of Edu-Checks. When the bank bills you, you write an Edu-Check (instead of a personal check) and mail it to the bank.

3. Insurance protection is effective upon receipt of the executed Edu-Check agreement. This insurance covers the amount of your line of credit. In the event of permanent disability or death, the student's education will continue to be paid by Edu-Check. (The amount of insurance decreases each month as you repay the principal.)

4. Each month you will receive a statement from Girard Bank, showing the amount of your principal monthly payment,

the amount of money in use for which you have written checks, the interest charge on this amount and the insurance premium.

The statement will also show the amount of money you have used to date and the amount of available credit that remains to pay education bills. If the remaining credit is insufficient to cover your education bills, this figure will alert you to the need to increase your line of credit.

5. Your first statement will arrive about forty-five days from the date you write your first Edu-Check. Subsequent statements will arrive on a monthly basis, in accord with the dates you have selected.

To determine the amount of the principal monthly payment you wish to make, divide the total amount of money you estimate you will need for the student's education by the number of monthly payments you have selected.

The principal monthly payment you establish will remain the same regardless of the amount of money you have in use at any one time. Only the interest and insurance charges will vary each month.

Edu-Check works like an ordinary checking account: You pay the college with an Edu-Check by the term or the semester, and you pay Girard Bank monthly.

Edu-Checks may be used for study in the United States or abroad, without notification to the bank.

You may establish a plan at any time during a student's education. You can arrange a plan for up to five years, or you can establish a line of credit for just one year of education expenses, to be repaid in twelve months.

The line of credit will automatically renew itself each year without reapplication.

The cost of Girard's Edu-Check Plan is low because interest is charged only on the amount of money you actually have in use.

The interest charge is 1 percent per month on an outstanding balance of $7,000 or less, plus 0.5 percent per month on any additional balance over $7,000.

The following table shows typical monthly payments for various amounts borrowed under the Edu-Check Plan. The pay-

Term of Education Expenses	Amount of Line of Credit	Number of Monthly Payments	Monthly Payments (principal only)
5 years	$15,000	96	$156.25
	15,000	60	250.00
4 years	12,000	96	125.00
	12,000	48	250.00
3 years	9,000	72	125.00
	9,000	36	250.00
2 years	6,000	48	125.00
	6,000	24	250.00
1 year	3,000	12	250.00
	2,000	12	166.67
	1,000	12	83.33

ments shown are repayments of principal only; they do not include finance charges.

For more information, write Girard Bank, 1339 Chestnut Street, Philadelphia, PA 19107.

Parents' Loan Plan of Princeton University

Recognizing the problems that face parents in paying for their children's college educations, some universities have established their own parents' loan plans. These plans are only for the parents of students who attend those universities. At Princeton, this plan supplements the established university program of financial aid.

Parents of enrolled or newly admitted students may apply for the plan, regardless of whether they qualify for financial aid.

Approval of these loans is based on the family's credit standing and the ability to repay. And the family that qualifies has up to 96 months to repay.

Who Is Eligible?

1. Loans are limited to parents who are citizens or permanent residents of the United States.

2. Parents of enrolled or admitted students may apply if their gross family income is at least $15,000 but not more than $60,000. (Where a gross family income is below $15,000, generally it will be more advantageous for the family to take advantage of Princeton's student financial aid programs.)

3. Approval of the loan will be based on the applicants' credit history and the ability to meet the repayment terms.

Interest will be charged at an annual rate of 8.75 percent, calculated daily on the outstanding balance. The rate will remain unchanged throughout the term of the loan, and it will apply to any additional borrowing that may be approved later.

Parents can borrow an amount up to the total cost of tuition, room and board, less any financial aid awarded to the student.

For each year's borrowing, two years are allowed for repayment. Thus the parents of freshmen who borrow each year will repay their loans over 96 months.

To apply for this loan, or for further information, write Princeton Parents' Loan Plan, Office of the Controller, P.O. Box 35, Princeton, NJ 08534. The deadline for application is June 15 preceding the semester the student will enroll.

The following table shows the amounts of the monthly payments and the total costs, including finance charges and insurance for various loans under the Princeton Parents' Loan Plan.

Annual Amount Borrowed	Total Amount Borrowed Over 4 Years	Total Monthly Payments for 96 Months	Total of All Payments
$1,000	$ 4,000	$ 51.70	$ 4,963.20
1,500	6,000	77.55	7,444.80
2,000	8,000	103.40	9,926.40
2,500	10,000	129.25	12,408.00
3,000	12,000	155.10	14,889.00
3,500	14,000	180.95	17,371.20
4,000	16,000	206.81	19,853.76
4,500	18,000	232.66	22,335.36
5,000	20,000	258.51	24,816.96
5,500	22,000	284.36	27,298.56

Parents' loan programs have been offered by banks, insurance companies and colleges for many years, enabling thousands of students to attend college.

Numerous parents' loan programs are available throughout the United States; the wise parent will look at several different plans to find the one that is most advantageous.

11

Student Employment in College Work Programs

There is continuing controversy over whether or not students should work while attending college.

Some educators believe that having a job detracts from a student's academic achievements. They say that students should not work at all.

Others maintain that students who work are more a part of the academic community; they have more responsibility and apply themselves to studying to a greater degree than do students who do not work.

The studies we have seen support those who believe that employed students do a better job academically. Since their study time is limited, they must organize that time better.

The College Work-Study Program

The main source of money for student employment has been the College Work-Study Program. Under this program, the federal government each year grants funds to colleges so that they can pay students who work for them. All of the jobs involved are part-time jobs (not more than 20 hours per week).

The College Work-Study Program is the largest student employment operation at most colleges. Students are usually offered one of these jobs as part of their financial aid package.

Who Is Eligible to Participate?

1. A student must exhibit financial need. The Financial Aid officer then decides which students are worthy of receiving a College Work-Study award.

2. A student must show sufficient academic excellence for holding a job and doing well academically.

3. A student must be a citizen or a permanent resident of the United States. Those who have only student visas are ineligible.

4. A student must be accepted for enrollment or be enrolled at least half time at a qualifying college.

5. A student who is attending college at the direction of a church or religious order is ineligible.

6. A student who is in default in any federal loan program, or who owes the college money, is ineligible.

The working student usually files a report of the number of hours worked, validated by a supervisor, with the student employment office. The student is generally paid every two weeks. Unlike other financial aid programs, this one provides the student with cash in hand.

A student may work for federal, state, local or public agencies or private nonprofit organizations. But colleges have come to rely on students to run their campus organizations. Consequently, at most universities, few students work off campus. (Each college may have a different policy in this regard.)

A Handbook for Student Employees

At Rutgers—the State University, where I was director of financial aid for the six colleges and more than 40,000 students, we thought it would be useful to prepare a handbook that would explain the College Work-Study Program to those students who needed to work. The selections from our handbook that follow should answer any questions you may have about the program.

Introduction

Student employment at Rutgers has two primary purposes: to provide students with financial support and to provide assistance to the departments of the University in carrying out their day-to-day operation. Where possible, the Financial Aid Office attempts to place students in positions where the most beneficial experience related to the student's major field of study may be gained.

Job Opportunities

1. *Federal College Work-Study Program.* Students who receive a financial aid award from the University may be offered a job supported by College Work-Study funds. The funds for CWS employment are provided 80 percent by federal funds and 20 percent by University funds. University regulations provide that a student may not work more than 35 hours per week during vacation periods and 15 hours per week during class and exam periods. Combined federal and University CWS funds may be used for both employment on campus and employment off campus in private nonprofit and public agencies. Lists of agencies that have contracts for the employment of CWS students are available in the Financial Aid Offices.

2. *Non-CWS Student Employment (on Campus).* Departments using wages of labor funds or grant funds to hire students on a part-time or temporary basis must follow the University's procedures pertaining to pay rates and general employment practices. Since all student pay rates must be consistent, questions about job titles or pay rates should be referred to the Financial Aid Offices for resolution.

3. *Off-campus Jobs.* Individuals and businesses in the local communities often contact the University to hire students for part-time or temporary positions. These jobs are posted in the Financial Aid Offices for three weeks. After that time, jobs are automatically removed from the posting. If the employer requests that the posting be retained after three weeks, another

call must be made. The Financial Aid Offices may refuse to post jobs that are below the minimum wage or that appear to discriminate in any way.

4. *Other employment.*

a. Teaching and Graduate Assistantships. These positions are made available to graduate students and carry salaries as well as teaching and research responsibilities.

b. Resident Adviser and Preceptorships. Students interested in positions in the residence halls may contact the Dean of Students on the campus.

Procedures for College Work-Study Students

1. File the Rutgers University Application for Financial Aid and FAF (Financial Aid Form) or GAPSFAS by the announced deadline date.

2. When an award letter, including a College Work-Study job, is received, the following action must be taken to validate the award:

a. Accept the job—unless you accept the award by the date indicated in the letter, a job may not be available to you.

b. Make an appointment with the local Financial Aid Office for an employment referral interview.

c. If the student is referred to a department by the Financial Aid Office, an Employment Authorization Form (EAF) will be provided to that student to take to the interview. This form should be completed and signed by the department chairperson when the student is hired.

3. When the form has been completed, the student must fill out a W-4 form and submit his social security card to the Financial Aid Office to be copied.

4. Upon returning all necessary forms, students will be instructed on how to complete their Time Report Forms properly and will be given a Pay Schedule.

Rights of Student Employees

1. The College Work-Study student has the right to know the specified period of employment and the hourly salary rate

and has the right to see a written job description before accepting the position.

2. The student has the right to receive at least the minimum wage unless the institution has received permission from the government to pay subminimum wages.

3. The student has the right to expect fair and equal treatment from the supervisor.

4. Students who do not wish to continue in the positions in which they are placed may request different placements. A student may be placed in another position if an opening is available.

College Work-Study jobs at Rutgers are many and varied. The following are examples of job titles and some of the student jobs that fall under those titles.

Social and community action
   Group leader
   Case aid
   Contact representative

Health professions
   General aide
   Pharmacy assistant
   Nurse's aide
   Medical lab teaching assistant
   Medical lab assistant

Tutorial assistants
   Group study assistant
   Tutorial assistant

Teaching assistants
   Nursery supervisor
   Undergraduate teaching assistant
   Nursery attendant

Classroom assistants
   Classroom assistant
   (nonteaching)
   Audio-visual aids operator
   Course material developer
   Reader
   Grader

Research (nonlaboratory)
   Research assistants

Library and museum
   Library assistants

Student personnel
   Student personnel assistant
   Specialist

Business-related
   Accounting clerk
   Business office assistant

Students Who Created Their Own Financial Aid

As a financial aid director, I have met many students who, with a little ingenuity, made their own financial aid. They were students who came to me with problems they thought could not be solved and then, after some exploration, came up with unique solutions and created their own campus jobs.

The Weenie Company

Sarah F. liked to have hot dogs and sandwiches available in the evening while she studied, and her friends, knowing she had food on hand, dropped in regularly.

When Sarah ran out of money feeding her friends, she came to the Financial Aid Office for help. Of course, we couldn't support her free food program, but I suggested that, since she was such a good cook, she might try packaging her food and selling it in the dormitories.

So Sarah borrowed an old cart to transport the food, her friends lent her insulated containers for the hot dogs and sandwiches and every night she made the rounds with her weenies and sandwiches. Students came to look forward to not having to go out at night for a snack.

Net profit the first night was $10 for fifty sales, and she made $50 profit the first week, working five nights.

Then Sarah's weenie business started to boom. The second week her profits hit $100. Soon Sarah could not keep up with the demands for her food and still have time to study. She came back to the office again with a different problem—how was she to keep up with her business and still keep up with her studies?

The college had a student employment office; I suggested that she hire other students to help her distribute her food. And the business continued to boom as one student told another about the Weenie Girl. Sarah just does the cooking now; other students deliver the food.

The Bicycle Man

Frank M. came to the Financial Aid Office looking for the money to replace his bike. The bicycle was so old and in such poor condition that it no longer operated. Frank told me that he had repaired it so many times that he had practically built a new bicycle.

Frank needed $100 to buy a new bike, and we could not give him the money. But it occurred to me that if he was so proficient in repairing his old bicycle, he might make some money repairing other students' bicycles.

He decided to give the repair business a try. We lent him a cellar room to work in, and Frank hung out his sign declaring that The Bicycle Man was in business. He also announced the address of his new business in an ad in the student newspaper.

In the first week there was no business at all (the student newspaper had given the wrong address). Then business picked up, and soon Frank had the $100 he needed to buy his new bike.

At the bicycle shop the owner told Frank he was overstocked and offered him a good discount if he would purchase more than one bicycle. And the owner agreed to take the $100 as a deposit on two bicycles.

Frank advertised the bikes for sale at his shop, and in two weeks he had sold both bikes for $120 each, making a net profit of $20 per bike. With his repair business, he was now making over $70 a week.

Frank decided to buy more bikes to sell, and his repair business continued to grow. Selling bikes on campus provided a more convenient way for students to purchase bikes at lower cost.

The Christmas Wreath Business

When my wife worked in the history department at Princeton, she looked forward to helping to decorate the offices for the Christmas holidays. One bright morning a few weeks before Christmas, two students came by, lugging a huge Christmas wreath. They were members of a group of students in the Christmas wreath business, and they were taking orders.

The wreath was beautiful—perfect for the door of the history department—and the head of the department ordered one. Meanwhile, other members of the department were deciding that they could use such pretty wreaths at home, and they placed orders, too.

The wreath merchants visited every department at the university, sold hundreds of Christmas wreaths and made hundreds of dollars.

The Birthday Cake Agency

Once when our daughter was in college, we decided to send her a birthday cake. The thought was appropriate, but the cake arrived in little pieces, which her roommates helped her eat with a spoon. And we never tried that again.

However, some bright students decided that a Birthday Cake Agency could fill a real demand. After all, it is impractical for parents to mail a cake, and most students don't have the time, the facilities or the inclination to bake birthday cakes.

Securing the addresses of the students' parents from the university, the cake merchants invited parents to place an order for the delivery of a cake on a student's birthday. The student manager, who is responsible for the operation of the agency and bought the cakes at a local bakery, insured that the cake would be delivered on the right day.

The House Plant Agency

A student who loved house plants brought a number of them with her when she came to the university. Other students saw how cheerful the plants made her dormitory room appear and asked if they couldn't buy some.

After she had sold quite a few plants at a profit, she decided there might be money to be made in selling plants.

So she visited the local florist, invested in some inexpensive pots and potting soil and proceeded to root cuttings. This soon provided her with new plants for sale. For this student, house plants brightened not only her room but her pocketbook.

At Princeton University, there are approximately fifty student-operated agencies that consistently produce money for students. The brief list that follows suggests the range of these student-managed operations.

Athletic shoes and supplies	News—*New York Times* delivery	Sportswear
Bagels	Parking	Stereos
Beer mugs	Photos	Sweaters
Clothing	Pinballs	T-shirts
Data	Pizza	Tennis ball sales
Ethnic food delivery	Racquet sales and restringing	Thesis binding
Freshman Herald Yearbook	Record sales	Typewriter and calculator sales
Furniture	Refrigerators	Typing
Linen	Ring sales	Umbrella sales
Magazines	Signs	Wall banner sales
	Souvenirs	Water beds

The formula for a successful student business involves finding a service that is needed and then filling that need. In this way, many students have paid for a large portion of their college expenses.

12

Financial Help for Women
in Special Circumstances

While most forms of federal and state financial assistance to students are awarded without regard for the recipient's sex, legislators are now beginning to provide for financial aid intended specifically for women in certain special circumstances.

The most difficult situation may be that of the married woman who has had no education beyond high school or has no marketable skills and who, after many years as a homemaker, suddenly finds her marriage ended by death, divorce or separation. Her need to earn an income may send her to college, and that same need may require that she have some amount of financial assistance to help meet the cost of her education.

The woman in this situation has been officially recognized as a displaced homemaker.

The displaced homemaker has been defined as a woman married at least five years and then widowed, divorced, separated or deserted; she is in need of financial help, whether she is presently employed or seeking employment.

The Displaced Homemakers legislation was passed by the 96th Congress as part of Title III of the Comprehensive Employment and Training Act (CETA). The bill, H.R. 10270, was sponsored originally by Representative Augustus Hawkins of California.

The Displaced Homemakers Bill was designed to establish a minimum of 50 centers (one in each state). These centers would provide employment training, counseling and teach job skills to women who have spent the greater part of their lives caring for homes, children and husbands. Due to the death of their spouses or divorce, they suddenly find themselves without any means of support and few marketable skills.

The U.S. Labor Department made a commitment of $5 million to the program, an average of $100,000 per center.

President Carter's budget proposed that the program's funding be reduced by half—to $2.5 million. Since there are an estimated 2.2 million displaced homemakers in the United States, this would mean slightly more than $1.00 per homemaker. Certainly, this cannot make much impact if these women are to be helped in the manner originally intended.

Specific appropriations for the program will be worked out in the summer and fall of 1979. It should be of interest to the displaced homemakers who are in need of this educational opportunity.

State Assistance for Displaced Homemakers

California has had a pilot project for displaced homemakers since 1975, when the state legislature established programs in Alameda and Los Angeles counties.

Educational programs include community college courses that offer college credit or lead to a high school equivalency certificate.

The director of the counseling centers has stressed that displaced homemakers need not only counseling for legal or health problems but also job counseling and financial aid to enable them to return to college or to update their job skills.

The California legislature appropriated $100,000 per year for two years for this program (1977–1979). Funding for the 1980s has not been resolved.

Delaware is hiring personnel in the Division of Vocational Rehabilitation to serve the needs of displaced homemakers.

At this writing, the programs include job counseling, job training and placement, financial management services, educational and health services and research for the creation of new jobs.

For further information, residents of Delaware may write

the State Department of Labor, Division of Vocational Rehabilitation, 1500 Shallcross Avenue, Wilmington, DE 19806.

At this writing, Delaware has not passed its displaced homemaker bill.

Maryland's displaced homemaker law states that the displaced homemaker must be at least thirty-five years of age and unemployment-prone because of a lack of formal job experience.

As of this writing, a displaced homemaker center in Baltimore, Maryland, has helped 800 women and has 300 more enrolled in its programs. The center also maintains a small library of pertinent information on job opportunities for women.

The Baltimore center has found that the need for financial aid is so pressing in some cases that it has had to provide money for transportation to enable women to take courses they need.

The Maryland law was scheduled to expire in the spring of 1979. If the funds were not forthcoming to continue their programs, the center planned to seek community support.

Massachusetts has a Homemaker Re-Entry Program, a pilot project in Gardner, Massachusetts, funded by the federal Comprehensive Employment and Training Act (CETA).

Massachusetts also has a bill pending that would establish displaced homemaker centers throughout the state.

The CETA program provides job counseling, training leading to a high school equivalency certificate, workshops that provide financial aid information, job search workshops and temporary placement. At the conclusion of the program, individuals may enroll in other CETA training programs or may take a one-year job placement in a PSC position.

Minnesota has passed legislation establishing displaced homemaker centers in Minneapolis–St. Paul and one rural area. The service programs were to include financial counseling, job counseling, job training and job placement.

This is another pilot program; it was scheduled to expire in 1979.

Nebraska has established a displaced homemaker center in Omaha and was to establish another center in a county of more than 30,000 population.

The aim of the Nebraska program is to provide displaced homemakers with the necessary counseling, training, skills and referral services to become gainfully employed and independent.

Oregon's displaced homemaker center in Eugene makes its services available to all state residents. Educational services include community college courses for credit or leading to a high school equivalency certificate.

The Oregon act was scheduled to expire in June 1979.

Ohio appropriated $200,000 for a two-year pilot displaced homemaker center at Cuyahoga Community College in Cleveland. Its services are available to all state residents.

Educational opportunities include community college courses for credit or leading to a high school equivalency certificate. The act will expire in July 1980.

Texas has established a displaced homemaker center in Dallas–Fort Worth, and another will be located in a county whose population is less than 100,000.

This Displaced Homemaker Act is not a statewide program; it is limited to the two service centers. Job training and counseling will be available, and financial aid will be offered to those who continue their education with the purpose of training for employment.

The Texas legislature appropriated $200,000 for the pilot program; the act will expire August 31, 1981.

The listing that follows reports the status of displaced homemaker legislation in various states, as of 1978.

Alabama
No plans for legislation.

Alaska
Bill under development.

Arkansas
No plans for legislation.

Arizona
Bill submitted, not passed.

California
Centers in operation in Alameda and Los Angeles counties.

Colorado
Bill passed but not yet implemented.

Delaware
Bill has been reintroduced.

Florida
Bill passed, but no funding is available.

Georgia
Bill under development.

Hawaii
Bill in planning in the Commission on the Status of Women.

Idaho
Bill to be introduced.

Illinois
Bill passed but not yet implemented.

Indiana
No plans for legislation.

New Jersey
Legislature has appropriated $25,000 for 1979–80 to study needs of displaced homemakers.

New Mexico
Bill submitted and under consideration.

New York
CETA-funded center in operation as an educational training center.

North Carolina
No plans for legislation.

North Dakota
Bill under development.

Ohio
Center in operation.

Oklahoma
Bill under consideration.

Oregon
Center in operation.

Pennsylvania
Bill scheduled to be reintroduced.

Puerto Rico
No plans for legislation.

Rhode Island
Bill under consideration.

South Carolina
No plans for legislation.

South Dakota
Bill under development.

Tennessee
No plans for legislation.

Texas
Center in operation.

Utah
No plans for legislation.

Vermont
No plans for legislation.

Virgin Islands
No plans for legislation.

Virginia
No plans for legislation.

Washington
Bill not yet passed.

West Virginia
No plans for legislation.

Wisconsin
Bill submitted and under consideration.

Clearly, displaced homemaker legislation is still very much in its infancy. Where legislation is expiring and where new bills are pending, those who want to help the displaced homemaker should write their state legislators and their representatives in Congress in support of the legislation.

Scholarship Assistance for Women from Business and Professional Organizations

The Business and Professional Women's Foundation

Established by the National Federation of Business and Women's Clubs, the Business and Professional Women's Foundation of Washington, D.C., provides educational assistance to women through grants, fellowships and scholarships. To date, a total of $805,000 in scholarships for career training has been awarded to 2,360 women.

Scholarships are awarded for the training of women over twenty-five years of age for employment or advancement in a business or professional field.

Scholarship awards are determined by the applicant's financial need, her career potential and her plan for using the training in career development.

The scholarships are granted for one year, and reapplication for additional years may be made. The maximum award in any one year is $1,000.

The foundation also administers four scholarship programs for job-related education for mature women: the Clairol Loving Care Scholarships, the BPW Career Advancement Scholarships, the Florence Morse Scholarships and the Kelly Services Second Career Scholarships.

These scholarships are awarded for full-time or part-time programs of study, and they may cover academic or vocational training.

All four scholarships may be sought at the same time on the same official application form. To obtain a copy, write Business and Professional Women's Foundation, 2012 Massachusetts Avenue, N.W., Washington, D.C. 20036.

The Clairol Loving Care Scholarship

The Clairol Loving Care Scholarship program is one of the few nationwide, company-sponsored scholarship programs for women over thirty. Established in 1973, it has awarded an estimated $250,000 in scholarships to approximately 700,000 women.

This is one of the few scholarship funds that subsidizes both full-time and part-time students—an important consideration for working women who can only pursue their education part time.

Scholarship recipients are selected by the Business and Professional Women's Foundation on the basis of need, merit, relevancy of studies to career goals and attainment of those goals within a reasonable amount of time.

The BPW Career Advancement Scholarship

The BPW Career Advancement Scholarship is awarded to women who are at least twenty-five years of age, citizens of the United States and officially accepted for a program or course of study at an accredited educational institution in the United States.

The applicant is expected to furnish information concerning the cost of the specific course of study and her qualifications for taking the course.

Preference is given to those applicants who have a definite plan for using their training. The director of the BPW Foundation has indicated that the scholarships are awarded to women who are more likely to succeed in finding a job in the marketplace.

The BPW Foundation has been funded to do job studies, run management seminars and create an employment advisory to assure that its scholarship money will put women in the job market and not on the unemployment line.

The Florence Morse Scholarship

The Florence Morse Scholarship is another award for women who are at least twenty-five years of age. They must also be in their junior or senior year at a business school accredited by the American Assembly of Collegiate Schools of Business. This is a national scholarship, available to any woman who is a citizen of the United States.

When this scholarship is awarded, tuition and fees are paid directly to the school. Any additional amount awarded for expenses is paid directly to the recipient. Scholarships range from $100 to $1,000 for one year.

The Kelly Services Second Career Scholarship

Kelly Services Second Career Scholarships are awarded to women at least twenty-five years of age who have spent five years or more as full-time homemakers and who seek employment in business as a result of the death of a spouse or the dissolution of a marriage.

This scholarship, like the others administered by the BPW Foundation, cannot be used for study at the doctoral level, correspondence courses or study in a foreign country.

The value of the Kelly Services scholarship ranges from $100 to $1,000 for one year; the average award is between $200 and $500.

The Exxon Education Foundation Scholarship

The scholarship award of the Exxon Education Foundation is intended to help women over thirty, who are already working in support positions in the law and business fields, to attain full professional status.

Applicants must be admitted to a qualified school before applying to the financial aid officer for an Exxon scholarship. The decisions regarding recipients and amounts of the scholarships are made by the schools.

Grants of $84,000 to $100,000 have been made to the law schools of the University of California at Berkeley and the University of Chicago and the business school at Stanford to fund the scholarship program.

At Berkeley, the individual Exxon awards average about $3,000 each.

The Rotary Foundation Scholarship for Teachers of the Handicapped

The Rotary Foundation offers scholarships for women who intend to study in the field of the handicapped.

The applicant must be an experienced teacher, twenty-five to fifty years of age, at least a high school graduate (or the equivalent) and must have been a full-time teacher of the mentally, physically or educationally handicapped for at least two years at the time of application.

Application blanks can be obtained from your local Rotary club.

The Amelia Earhart Scholarship

The Amelia Earhart Scholarship is sponsored by Zonta International to support study and research by young women scientists; one of its goals is to improve the status of women.

The applicant must have earned a bachelor's degree in a discipline basic to one of the many aerospace-related sciences. The applicant must also have gained acceptance at a qualified graduate school and must show promise of original research potential.

For information, write Zonta International, 59 East Van Buren Street, Chicago, IL 60605.

Special Loan Opportunities for Women

If your state has no displaced homemaker legislation, if you can't qualify for a scholarship and if you don't have the money you need to take courses, it's all right to borrow.

The federal government is probably the best bet for women who need money to pay for their education. In the preceding chapters, we discussed the five major loan and grant programs that are available to both women and men.

The main difference between these loans and those "for women only" that we will now describe seems to be that the loans for women have a lower interest rate (generally 5 percent) than the federal loans (7 percent).

The Sears-Roebuck Foundation Loan

The Sears-Roebuck Foundation has made $300,000 in loans available to women who have been accepted for graduate degree programs or graduate courses of study at schools accredited on the graduate level by the American Assembly of Collegiate Schools of Business.

Women who qualify may obtain loans of up to $2,000 per year at 5 percent interest. Repayment of the loans is scheduled over a five-year period, beginning one year after graduation. This program is administered by the Business and Professional Women's Foundation.

The Loan Fund for Women in Engineering Studies

The Loan Fund for Women in Engineering Studies was established by the Business and Professional Women's Foundation with an initial grant of $100,000 from the Exxon Education Foundation. Approximately $80,000 in loans is given each year to women who have been accepted for study in engineering programs accredited by the Engineers Council for Professional Development.

The Loan Fund is designed to assist women in their final two years of an accredited engineering program, including undergraduate, refresher and conversion programs and graduate studies.

Special encouragement is offered to those women who have work experience in engineering or related technical fields and to those who have not recently worked in engineering but who are qualified, through past study, for training in engineering or engineering technology.

Women who qualify may obtain individual loans of up to $10,000. Interest of 5 percent per annum begins immediately on completion of the program, and interest and principal are payable in five equal installments, one each year for five years, commencing twelve months after completion of the program. Any amount of interest may be prepaid at any time without penalty.

Applicants must be United States citizens, have financial need and possess a written acceptance for undergraduate or graduate study in a program accredited by the Engineers Council for Professional Development. Borrowers must carry at least 6 credit hours or the equivalent during each semester for which a loan is granted.

Applicants must also show work experience or academic achievement indicating career motivation and the ability to complete the intended course of study.

Requests for application forms, information and all correspondence concerning the Loan Fund should be addressed to the Loan Fund for Women in Engineering Studies, Business and Professional Women's Foundation, 2012 Massachusetts Avenue, N.W., Washington, D.C. 20036.

The deadline each year is May 15.

U.S. Public Health Service Nursing Loan

The U.S. Public Health Service Nursing Loan Program is intended to increase the opportunities for the training of nurses of both sexes by assisting graduate schools of nursing to establish student loan funds for their students.

The low-interest, long-term loans are made to students who need assistance in order to pursue a course of study leading to a diploma in nursing, an associate degree in nursing or a bachelor's degree in nursing (or the equivalent).

You can also get a loan for a graduate degree in nursing.

The applicant must be enrolled or accepted for enrollment in a school of nursing, pursuing or expecting to pursue a full-time or half-time course of study leading to a specified degree.

Loans are available to applicants in the United States, Puerto Rico, the Virgin Islands, Guam, the Canal Zone, American Samoa and the Trust Territory of the Pacific Islands.

For information, write the U.S. Public Health Service, Student Assistance Branch (BHM, HRA), NIH Building 31, Room 4c-39, 9000 Rockville Pike, Bethesda, MD 20014.

The Diuguid Fellowships

The Diuguid Fellowship Program for mature women is designed for those whose career and professional goals have been deferred because of marriage or for other reasons.

The fellowships make funds available for one year of intensive retraining or concentrated study on a full-time or part-time basis.

The applicant must demonstrate that a year of formal study

or independent effort can benefit her directly in the pursuit of a career.

The applicant must be over twenty-one years of age, have had to interrupt her career, must demonstrate financial need and must be a resident of the southern region of the United States.

For information, write the Diuguid Fellowships, Suite 484, 795 Peachtree Street N.E., Atlanta, GA 30308.

Scholarship Opportunities
for Young Women

When Kylene Baker won the Miss America pageant in 1978, she gasped in disbelief and tears streamed down her face. As Miss America, she would receive not only $50,000 worth of personal appearance bookings but a $20,000 scholarship to the college of her choice.

She had spoken earlier about wanting to continue her work in fashion merchandising, having graduated from Virginia Tech with a major in apparel design and fashion merchandising. She planned to use her scholarship to get a master's degree in business administration.

And she was not the only happy young woman that night. As the nationwide television audience looked on, the other finalists radiated their pleasure at winning scholarships worth $15,000 for the first runner-up, $10,000 for the second runner-up, $7,000 for the third runner-up and $5,000 for the fourth runner-up. The five remaining finalists would each receive a $3,000 scholarship, and all the other contestants had won at least a $1,000 scholarship.

The Miss America Foundation

The Miss America Foundation began awarding scholarships in 1945 when Miss New York City, Bess Myerson, was crowned Miss America. It is now the largest scholarship foundation distributing scholarships exclusively to young women; it gives $250,000 annually at the local, state and national levels.

But no young woman has to be a Miss America contestant to win a scholarship!

The lion's share of financial aid for women takes the form of scholarships for young women because the majority of women students enter college directly from high school.

In the following pages we detail a selection of the many scholarships specifically for young women that we think particularly valuable. (You can find information about hundreds more in your library, in your guidance counselor's office and in college catalogues.)

Athletic Scholarships

In 1978 an estimated 10,000 women from about 460 schools received athletic scholarships worth more than $7 million.

The cause of women who seek athletic scholarships is being helped substantially by a section of the Education Amendments Act passed by Congress in 1972: Title IX forbids sex discrimination in any educational institution that receives federal funds, and the prohibition applies on the athletic field as well as in the classroom. The Department of Health, Education and Welfare can deny federal funds to any institution that does not measure up. (Together, the nation's colleges receive approximately $12.2 billion annually from the federal government.)

Title IX has forced colleges to upgrade their women's athletic programs. In 1972, the budget for women's intercollegiate sports was only 1 percent of that for men's intercollegiate sports. Today, women's programs are receiving a sum that is about 18 percent of the amount being spent on men's programs. Thus there are now more athletic scholarships for women.

In 1979 the University of Michigan is expected to award thirty women's athletic scholarships at a cost of $100,000. In 1973 the university had only informal athletics for women; today it has ten varsity teams to the men's eleven.

At North Carolina State, athletic scholarships for women increased from none to forty-nine in four years; their cost has reached $300,000.

UCLA, with a national championship team led by Ann Meyers, will have a women's athletic budget of $527,000 in 1979. National television coverage of AIAW (Association for Intercollegiate Athletics for Women) championship basketball is further aiding the cause of women's sports and adding to the value of women's athletic scholarships.

Yale is another school making great strides in varsity women's sports: its athletic budget for women will be more than $600,000 in 1979—the largest in the nation. Twelve of Yale's fourteen varsity women's teams had winning seasons in 1979.

In 1971–1972, with 278 member schools, the Association for Intercollegiate Athletics for Women was formed. In 1978, the AIAW had 825 active members. Seventeen sports are contested under AIAW aegis, and it estimates that more than 100,000 women compete in intercollegiate sports.

We are beginning to hear stories of coaches luring women athletes to their campuses with offers of large scholarships, cars and living expenses—not only for basketball, but for such sports as lacrosse and soccer.

If you are a star on a high school team, don't overlook the possibility of an athletic scholarship. It could mean a lot of money to you and your family.

Ethnic Scholarships

The Daughters of Penelope

The Daughters of Penelope National Scholarships are open only to women of Greek ancestry (or women related to a Daughter of Penelope member). A recipient must remain single during her college tenure to qualify for renewal. This is one of many scholarships available to ethnic groups and typical of those restricted to persons of a specific national origin.

Applicants for this scholarship must be residents of the United States, Canada, Greece or some other country where there is an established Daughters of Penelope chapter. An applicant must rank high in her graduating class, have high SAT scores and establish leadership qualities in extracurricular activities.

Financial need is considered only when a choice must be made between two women of otherwise equal standing.

For information, write the chairman of the Scholarship Committee, Daughters of Penelope Senior Ladies Auxiliary, Grand Lodge, 1422 K Street, N.W., Washington, D.C. 20005.

United Negro College Fund

Although the prime purpose of the United Negro College Fund is to act as a fund-raiser for forty-one member institutions, some donors choose to earmark their contributions for scholarships to black students with financial need. UNCF scholarship money is expected to grow rapidly in the wake of the launching of its first full-scale Student Aid Program in 1977. While available to both women and men, it is the largest source of funds for black females.

In 1978, more than $300,000 in scholarship money was raised.

In Pennsylvania, a statewide payroll deduction program raised $95,663.11 for the UNCF Pennsylvania State Scholarship Fund. This sum provides scholarship money to black students who are Pennsylvania residents.

Public high schools in Delaware, New York City and Birmingham, Alabama, hold rap sessions to familiarize students with the UNCF scholarships. Students in these cities should check with their guidance counselors for time and place or write the United Negro College Fund, 500 East 62nd Street, New York, NY 10021.

In other parts of the country, students who want further information should either write to the above address or contact one of the area offices of the United Negro College Fund. Area offices are located in twenty-five cities:

Atlanta, Georgia
Birmingham, Alabama
Boston, Massachusetts
Chicago, Illinois
Cleveland, Ohio
Columbus, Ohio
Dallas, Texas
Daytona Beach, Florida
Detroit, Michigan
Denver, Colorado
Houston, Texas
Los Angeles, California
Milwaukee, Wisconsin

Minneapolis, Minnesota
Newark, New Jersey
New Haven, Connecticut
New Orleans, Louisiana
New York, New York
Norfolk, Virginia
Philadelphia, Pennsylvania
Portland, Oregon
St. Louis, Missouri
San Francisco, California
Seattle, Washington
Washington, D.C.

The United Negro College Fund does not process applications for financial assistance or administer these funds. Students who seek scholarships, loans, fellowships or work-study opportunities must write to the director of financial aid at the college they wish to attend.

Forty-one colleges are members of the United Negro College Fund and receive funds annually to supplement their programs of financial assistance for students. In 1978 the tuition at these colleges ranged from $600 to $2,250.

Alabama
> Oakwood College, Huntsville
> Stillman College, Tuscaloosa
> Talladega College, Talladega
> Tuskegee Institute, Tuskegee
> Miles College, Birmingham

Arkansas
> Philander Smith College, Little Rock

Florida
> Bethune-Cookman College, Daytona Beach
> Florida Memorial College, Miami

Georgia
> Atlanta University, Atlanta
> Clark College, Atlanta
> Interdenominational Theological Center, Atlanta
> Morehouse College, Atlanta
> Morris Brown College, Atlanta
> Paine College, Augusta
> Spelman College, Atlanta

Louisiana
> Dillard University, New Orleans
> Xavier University, New Orleans

Mississippi
> Rust College, Holly Springs
> Tougaloo College, Tougaloo

North Carolina
Barber-Scotia College, Concord
Bennett College, Greensboro
Johnson C. Smith University, Charlotte
Livingstone College, Salisbury
Saint Augustine's College, Raleigh
Shaw University, Raleigh

Ohio
Wilberforce University, Wilberforce

South Carolina
Benedict College, Columbia
Claflin College, Orangeburg
Voorhees College, Denmark

Tennessee
Fisk University, Nashville
Knoxville College, Jackson
LeMoyne-Owen College, Memphis

Texas
Bishop College, Dallas
Huston-Tillotson College, Austin
Jarvis Christian College, Hawkins
Paul Quinn College, Waco
Texas College, Tyler
Wiley College, Marshall

Virginia
St. Paul's College, Lawrenceville
Virginia Union University, Richmond

The following colleges offer Food Fair Scholarships:

University of Connecticut
Delaware State College
University of Florida
Jacksonville University, Florida
University of Miami, Florida
Florida State University
University of South Florida
Florida Memorial College

Miami-Dade Community College, Florida
Johns Hopkins University, Maryland
Loyola College, Maryland
University of Maryland
Valdosta State College, Georgia
University of Georgia
Fairleigh Dickinson University, New Jersey
Rutgers University, New Jersey
Seton Hall University, New Jersey
Cornell University, New York
Fordham University, New York
College of William and Mary, Virginia
Delaware Valley College, Pennsylvania
Drexel University, Pennsylvania
La Salle College, Pennsylvania
Lincoln University, Pennsylvania
University of Pennsylvania
Pennsylvania State University
Saint Joseph's College, Pennsylvania
Temple University, Pennsylvania
Villanova University, Pennsylvania

The maximum value of these scholarships varies from $1,000 to $2,000.

Firestone Tire and Rubber Company Scholarship

The Firestone Tire and Rubber Company Scholarship pays up to $1,500 per academic year when the student attends a local or state college or university and up to $3,000 per year when the student attends a private college or university.

The scholarship is limited to children of employees of the Firestone Tire and Rubber Company. Forty new scholarships are granted each year, plus renewals of existing scholarships. The scholarship may be renewed for a total of four years (contingent on satisfactory scholastic and personal records).

Public Service Scholarships

The Truman Scholarship

The Truman Scholarship was established by Congress as a memorial Harry S. Truman Scholarship to former President Harry S. Truman. It provides four-year college scholarships for young women and men who demonstrate a serious intent to pursue careers in public service.

Applicants for a Truman Scholarship must exhibit academic and citizenship traits of the highest calibre and must be citizens of the United States.

One scholar will be selected from each state, the District of Columbia and Puerto Rico. The Virgin Islands, American Samoa, Guam and the Trust Territory of the Pacific Islands will be considered as an entity for the award of one additional scholarship.

For information, write to the Truman Scholarship Foundation, 712 Jackson Place, N.W., Washington, D.C. 20006.

Scholarship for a Degree in Architecture

This scholarship is intended for students from minority and/or disadvantaged backgrounds who would not otherwise have the opportunity to enroll in architectural studies.

The applicant must be a high school graduate; students in junior college or technical schools are eligible.

Candidates must be sponsored by one of the following: An individual architect or firm, a guidance counselor, the dean or administrative head of an accredited school of architecture or the director of a community or civic organization.

A recipient must be admitted to an accredited school of architecture before accepting the award. For information, write the Director, Education Programs, American Institute of Architects, 1735 New York Avenue N.W., Washington, D.C. 20006.

The Rotary Foundation Scholarships

The Rotary offers scholarships in the United States and 150 other countries. Their field of study is unrestricted; three months of intensive language training is provided for scholarship winners who wish to study outside their own country.

Applicants for a Rotary scholarship must be eighteen to twenty-four years of age and unmarried and must have completed at least two years of university-level work (or the equivalent) but must not have a B.A. at the date study begins.

For further information, write your nearest Rotary Club.

Academic Scholarships

The National Merit Scholarship

The National Merit Scholarships are well known to most high school seniors. They are based on academic excellence and/or financial need.

To win a merit scholarship, you must take the PSAT test, usually in October of your junior year. Your performance on this test will qualify you as a semifinalist. Then all semifinalists must take the SAT, usually in November of your senior year. Your score on this test determines whether or not you are a finalist.

Three types of scholarships are awarded.

1. Some scholarships are based solely on merit (financial need is not taken into consideration). These scholarships are worth $1,000; approximately 1,000 are given for one year.

2. Some colleges sponsor national awards. These are based on financial need and range between $100 and $1,500 for four years. Contact the college you wish to attend to learn whether or not they sponsor this scholarship.

3. Some corporations sponsor national merit awards that are worth $250 to $1,500 per year and are based on financial need. These awards are good for four years. Your parents should contact their employers to find out whether or not they sponsor national merit scholarships.

The Air Force ROTC Scholarship Program for Women

A woman Air Force ROTC graduate with a bachelor's degree will be commissioned as a second lieutenant in the Air Force. Her career field will be based on many factors: the needs of the Air Force, educational pursuits and personal interests. All career fields are open to women except pilot, navigator and missile operations (which are considered combat specialties).

Many scholarships are offered in the fields of science, electronic engineering, computer science and other highly technical and mechanical areas. The Air Force encourages women to prepare for entry by selecting academic majors that include math, science or engineering.

Once commissioned as a second lieutenant and called to active duty with the Air Force, women receive the same pay, benefits and promotion opportunities as men.

For information, write the Air Force ROTC, P.O. Box AF, Peoria, IL 61614.

The scholarships for women described in this chapter are

among the most interesting local, national and international scholarships for women. The details of many more will be found at your library, your guidance counselor's office and in college catalogues.

14

Scholarships for Boy Scouts and Girl Scouts

A variety of college scholarship awards are available to students who have achieved various ranks in the Boy Scouts and Girl Scouts organizations.

Many of these scholarships are offered only at specific colleges. Following is a list of colleges offering these scholarships.

Grand Canyon College, Phoenix, Arizona

A President's grant is given in the amount of $300 per year, renewable for three years, to any Scout achieving the Eagle rank and enrolling in Grand Canyon College.

For information, write the Director of Financial Aid, Grand Canyon College, 3330 West Camelback Road, Phoenix, AZ 85017.

Johnson and Wales College, Providence, Rhode Island

The Gaebe Eagle Scout Award amounts to $500 annually. You must be an Eagle Scout, you must have received the religious award of your faith, and you must meet the admission requirements of Johnson and Wales College. You do not have to meet any other specifications for this scholarship.

For information, write the Financial Aid Officer, Johnson and Wales College, Abbott Place, Providence, RI 02903.

New Mexico Military Institute, Roswell, New Mexico

A scholarship of $2,000 ($1,000 for each of two years) is available to a member of the Eagle Scout Association. Applicants must be single, male, under twenty-six and must meet college standards.

For information, write the Assistant Dean, New Mexico Military Institute, Roswell, NM 88201.

Springfield College, Springfield, Massachusetts

An annual award is given to an outstanding Scout with the highest ideal of Scouting who wishes to train for professional leadership in boys' work at Springfield College. The scholarship is worth $800 to $1,200 on a year-to-year basis; students already holding scholarships are given preference over new applicants.

For information, write the Director of Financial Aid, Springfield College, Springfield, MA 01109.

Rose-Hulman Institute, Terre Haute, Indiana

The Forrest G. Shere Honorary Scout Scholarship is awarded to a high school senior active in Scouting. This scholarship, worth $400, is awarded by June 1. To be eligible, you must have been accepted to the Rose Polytechnic Institute prior to March 15.

For information, write the Scout Executive, 501 South 25th Street, Terre Haute, IN 47803.

Stanford University, Stanford, California

Stanford awards the Dofflemyer Honors Scholarships to Eagle Scouts residing in Arizona, California, Hawaii, Nevada, Utah and Rock Springs, Wyoming.

This scholarship is based on financial need and the recommendation of the Scout Executive. Applicants must indicate on the Financial Aid form of the Educational Testing Service that they wish to be considered for this scholarship.

Proof of Eagle rank has to be sent directly to the Financial Aid Office, Stanford University, Stanford CA 94305.

Upsala College, East Orange, New Jersey

The Alpha Phi Omega Fraternity established a scholarship to be awarded annually to a member of the freshman class who has distinguished himself in Scouting and in his studies.

For information, write Upsala College, East Orange, NJ 07019.

Wesleyan University, Middletown, Connecticut

You must be an Eagle Scout and show financial need; you must have a B average. This award is given for outstanding citizenship.

For information, write the Financial Aid Office, North College, Wesleyan University, Middletown, CT 06457.

Whittier College, Whittier, California

The Gifford Eagle Scout Scholarships are awarded to Eagle Scouts who must secure an education through their own efforts and who plan a career in youth leadership, professional Scouting or the ministry. The grants amount to $500 to $800 per year.

Whittier College also grants the George E. Wanberg Scholarship to young men who plan careers in youth leadership, Scouting, YMCA and other youth-serving agencies. This scholarship is worth $200 to $800 per year, and it is renewable.

Write directly to the college for applications for these scholarships.

Charles McG. Sweitzer Scout Scholarship Funds

These scholarships are awarded to Scouts or former Scouts of the National Capital Area Council. Applicants must have been accepted by a college or university; eligibility will be determined by a committee of veteran Scouts.

For information, write the Scout Service Center, 9190 Wisconsin Avenue, Washington, D.C. 20014.

Carter Scholarship Grants for New England Scouts

The Marjorie Sells Carter Scholarships are designed to assist young men living in the New England states who have been members of the Boy Scouts of America for at least two years. Applicants must show promise of future leadership and must exhibit financial need.

This scholarship awards $1,000 to $3,000, as recommended by the financial aid officer of the applicant's college. Applicants must present a letter of recommendation from the Scout Council Executive and recommendations from their high school guidance councelor.

For information, write the Boy Scouts of America, North Brunswick, NJ 08902, or individual Scout Councils in New England.

Eisenhower Memorial Scholarship Foundation

Four-year scholarships of $8,000 each are available to high school seniors who have never attended college.

Applicants are judged on scholastic performance, leadership potential and their promise of becoming opinion leaders; applicants must have faith in a Divine Being and a firm belief in the free enterprise system and the American way of life.

This scholarship is highly competitive and is limited to certain Indiana colleges. Financial need is not a consideration.

For information, write the Eisenhower Memorial Scholarship Foundation, P.O. Box 1324, Bloomington, IN 47401.

J. Edgar Hoover Scholarships

These scholarships are awarded to Explorer Scouts active in a post specializing in law enforcement. The applicant must be a high school senior, under twenty-one years of age. The scholarship awards tuition only.

For information, write the Boy Scouts of America, Exploring Division, North Brunswick, NJ 08902.

James S. Kemper Foundation Scholarships

Scholarships are available to Explorer Scouts who pursue a career related to the insurance field; they provide tuition assistance at foundation-approved colleges and universities.

For information, write Kemper Insurance Center, Long Grove, IL 60049.

The Pickard Scholarship

This scholarship is awarded to an Explorer Scout in the Delaware-Maryland-Virginia Council who has been recommended by his scout executive and approved by the scholarship committee.

Preference is given to Scout applicants who have attained Eagle rank or Explorers who have distinguished records. The scholarship may be renewed annually.

For information, write the Del-Mar-Va Council, Eighth and Washington Streets, Wilmington, DE 19801.

The Rev. Robert B. Parker Memorial Fund, Peabody, Massachusetts

This is a fund of $40,000, the income to be used for scholarship grants. Four-fifths of the amount is earmarked to assist worthy and needy Scouts of the North Bay, Massachusetts, Council to obtain a college education. Scholarship grants may be repaid when income makes it possible.

For information, write the North Bay Council, Boy Scouts of America, Scouting Way, Peabody MA 01960.

Scouting Career Scholarship Fund, New York, New York

These scholarships of $1,000 per year are awarded on an annual basis to New York City Scouts by a special scholarship committee appointed by the Greater New York Councils Executive Board. The scholarships are intended specifically for students who plan careers as professional Scout leaders.

Eligibility is determined by financial need and service on the Greater New York Councils summer camp staff in the year the scholarship is to take effect.

For information, write the Scholarship Coordinator, Boy Scouts of America, 345 Hudson Street, New York, NY 10014.

Mervyn R. Blacow Scholarship Fund, Sacramento, California

This scholarship of $500 is awarded annually to deserving Eagle Scouts residing in the Golden Empire Council, Sacramento, California. Preference will be given to those who show a strong interest in professional Scouting as their life's career. Applicants must exhibit a need for financial help to attend college.

For information, write the Eagle Scout Association, Golden Empire Council, Boy Scouts of America, P.O. Box 254946, Sacramento, CA 95825.

Lou Henry Hoover Girl Scout Scholarship

Among the scholarships available to Senior Girl Scouts is one administered by Temple University. Applicants must be graduating high school seniors who plan to attend Temple's Ambler campus.

To qualify, you must be a Girl Scout planning to study landscape design and horticulture, you must have completed five consecutive years of responsible participation in the Girl Scout program immediately prior to applying for the scholarship, you must have high scholastic achievement, you must present personal recommendations and your leadership must be of the highest calibre.

For information, write the Department of Horticulture and Landscape Design, Temple University, Ambler, Pennsylvania 19002.

Preparatory School Scholarships for Boy Scouts

Several preparatory schools award scholarship money to Boy Scouts.

The Choate School, Wallingford, Connecticut

Scholarships of $5,000 and over are awarded to Scouts and Explorers entering Choate in grades 9–12. The scholarships are based on financial need and are open to all boys on recommendation by the local Scout Executive.

For information, write the Scholarship Chairman, The Choate School, Wallingford, CT 06492.

Culver Military Academy, Culver, Indiana

Scholarships are available annually to Scouts or Explorers who must have completed 8th, 9th and 10th grades. The amount of the scholarship will depend on financial need.

For information, write the Dean of Admissions, Culver Military Academy, Culver, IN 46511.

Howe Military School, Howe, Indiana

A scholarship award is available annually to Scouts or Explorers entering Howe. The amount of the scholarship is determined by financial need.

For information, write the Director of Admissions, Howe Military School, Howe, IN 46746.

15

The ROTC Programs Offer Four-year Scholarships Worth up to $33,000

The single largest scholarship for men and women is the one presented by the Army, the Navy and Marine Corps and the Air Force ROTC programs. An ROTC scholarship can be worth $33,000 for four years.

The Army ROTC Program

The Army Reserve Officers' Training Corps provides military leadership instruction at more than 285 colleges and universities throughout the nation. The program develops selected men and women for positions of responsibility as officers in the active Army and its Reserve.

Army ROTC is traditionally a four-year program that consists of a basic and an advanced course. However, it also offers a two-year program that enables junior college and community college students and those who missed ROTC in their first two years of college to qualify for a commission.

At present the Army has a total of 6,500 ROTC scholarships in effect.

This scholarship pays for college tuition, textbooks, laboratory fees and other purely academic expenses. Scholarship recipients also get a tax-free subsistence allowance of $100 a month for up to ten months of each school year that the scholarship is in effect.

The four-year ROTC scholarship can be worth between $10,000 and $33,000 for a four-year course of study.

Who Is Eligible for an Army ROTC Scholarship?

Applicants for an Army ROTC scholarship must be citizens of the United States and seventeen years of age before the scholarship becomes effective.

Applicants must have taken, or be scheduled to take, either the SAT or the American College Test, not later than the November test dates of the year they apply for the scholarship.

Applicants must be high school graduates or have equivalent credit, and they must meet specified physical standards.

Applicants must be able to complete all requirements for a commission and a college degree and still be under twenty-five years of age on June 30 of the year they become eligible for appointment as officers.

Applicants agree to accept either a Regular Army or Army Reserve commission and to serve on active duty for at least four years. Should their Regular Army commission be terminated early, applicants agree to accept an appointment in the Army Reserve.

The three-year and two-year ROTC scholarships are both awarded competitively to students who are enrolled in ROTC or who are eligible for advanced placement in ROTC, including those who are cross-enrolled.

Students who attend Basic Camp of the two-year program may compete for two-year scholarships.

ROTC Scholarships for Enlisted Personnel

Two-year scholarships are also available, on a competitive basis, to enlisted personnel on active duty.

They must meet the citizenship, age and physical requirements for four-year scholarship applicants, and they must have served at least one year on active duty so that they can be given credit for the Basic Course (the first two years of ROTC).

Enlisted personnel must have completed at least two years but not more than two and one-half years of college; they must be accepted as juniors (third-year students) by an institution offering Army ROTC.

Enlisted personnel who win scholarships will be discharged from active duty. They must then enlist immediately in the U.S. Army Reserve and sign an Army ROTC Financial Assistance Scholarship contract.

Application should be made between January 15 and April 15. For information, write Army ROTC Scholarships, Fort Monroe, VA 23651.

Military Obligation for Scholarship Winners

All ROTC scholarship students have a six-year military obligation—four years on active duty and two years in the Reserve.

In their senior year, cadets usually request the branches of the Army in which they would like to be commissioned. They indicate first, second, third and fourth choices. The needs of the Army are paramount here; however, most students are commissioned in one of their first two choices.

Assignments will usually reflect the personal goals, education and abilities of the individual. The Army provides many opportunities for officers to use the academic skills they acquire as college students.

Those who decide to make a career of the Army will have their security assured through one of the best retirement systems in the world. Army retirement can come after twenty years of active service, with an insured income of 50 percent of base pay. Various options assure survivors of a fixed income plus other benefits.

How Are Scholarship Winners Selected?

Army ROTC scholarship winners are selected on the basis of the results of their SAT or American College Test, personal interviews, high school academic record and extracurricular, leadership and athletic activities.

Students who do not have time for extensive participation in sports or extracurricular activities because they hold part-time jobs are awarded points based on the number of hours they work per week.

Scholarship students are expected to maintain acceptable standards of academic achievement, personal conduct and physical fitness. They must rank in the upper third of their Army ROTC class and demonstrate leadership potential.

Records will be reviewed each semester by the professor of military science to insure that each student is still eligible for continued financial aid.

The period for requesting application forms for four-year Army ROTC scholarships is April 1 through November 15.

Application forms and further information may be obtained by writing Army ROTC Scholarships, P.O. Box 12703, Philadelphia, PA 19134.

The Navy and Marine Corps ROTC Program

The Naval Reserve Officers' Training Corps offers young men and women the opportunity to qualify for commissions in the U.S. Navy Reserve while attending college.

The NROTC scholarship winner receives benefits worth as much as $25,000 at some of the country's leading universities, and later the Navy receives a career officer with a broad education. The program educates and trains qualified young men and women for careers as commissioned officers of the Regular Navy and the Marine Corps.

NROTC scholarships are similar to those offered by the Army.

Who Is Eligible for an NROTC Scholarship?

To be eligible for an NROTC scholarship, you must be a citizen of the United States and seventeen years of age by September of the year in which you apply.

Applicants must be high school graduates or possess an equivalent certificate, and they must be physically qualified in accordance with the standards prescribed for midshipmen.

Applicants must be willing to bear arms and support and defend the Constitution of the United States.

Applicants must be able to complete all requirements for a commission and a college degree, and they must be no more than twenty-one years of age on June 30 of the year they become eligible for appointment as officers. Applicants sign an agreement that provides for the requirements set forth in the following paragraph. (Students under eighteen must have their agreement signed by a parent or guardian.)

Applicants agree to pursue academic majors of interest to the Navy or the Marine Corps; to complete prescribed naval science courses, prescribed university courses, drills prescribed by the Navy and summer training periods; to accept a commission in the Regular Navy or Marine Corps if offered; and to serve a minimum of six years from the date of acceptance of the original commission.

The differences between the NROTC and the Army ROTC are these:

1. The maximum age at which you can be commissioned is twenty-one in the NROTC and twenty-five in the Army ROTC.

2. In the NROTC you must pursue prescribed academic courses of interest to the Navy or the Marine Corps.

3. You must serve six years of duty in the Navy or the Marine Corps as opposed to four years in the Army.

The Marine NROTC Program

The NROTC program is the largest single source of regular officers for the Marine Corps. There is room for only a limited number of midshipmen in the Marine program, and those who qualify for and complete the program receive a commission as an officer in the Marine Corps.

Marines participate in the same basic program as Navy NROTC midshipmen for the first two years. In keeping with the tradition of the Marines, they are authorized to wear the eagle, glove and anchor on their midshipmen uniforms, and they participate in Marine-oriented activities at the unit.

Marine midshipmen pursue courses of study that range from engineering to the liberal arts. Beginning in the junior year, Marine midshipmen are taught Marine-oriented naval science courses.

In the summer that follows their junior year, Marine midshipmen report to Quantico, Virginia, for six weeks of pre-commission training. This session provides an intensive introduction to the Marine Corps and a chance for students to measure themselves against Marine midshipmen from schools across the country.

Upon successful completion of their senior year, Marine midshipmen are commissioned as second lieutenants in the Marine Corps.

Course Requirements for NROTC Students

The courses that NROTC students are required to take may vary somewhat among colleges. The amount of credit toward the B.A. degree that these courses earn also varies among educational institutions and the academic departments within them.

Nevertheless, all NROTC students should expect to take the following courses, regardless of their academic majors:

> Introduction to Naval Science
> Naval Ships Systems
> Seapower and Maritime Affairs
> Navigation and Naval Operations
> Leadership and Management
> American Military Affairs (History)
> National Security Policy (Political Science)
> Calculus (two semesters)
> Physics (two semesters)

Midshipmen must complete all requirements for a B.A. degree, in accordance with university rules and regulations, *as well as* courses specified by the Navy.

Marine midshipmen may normally enroll in any four-year course of study leading to a B.A. degree.

Students may enroll in a five-year course of study for a B.A. degree, provided they will not have reached their twentieth birthday on June 30 of the calendar year in which they will complete their fifth year and be commissioned. In this case, the student is granted a one-year leave of absence, without compensation or benefits, in order to qualify for such a degree.

What Are the NROTC Physical Standards?

The height requirements for male students are 62 to 78 inches (Navy) and 66 to 78 inches (Marines). For women students, the requirements are 60 to 78 inches (Navy) and 60 to 78 inches (Marines). The weight requirement is proportionate to the individual's height.

Vision must be 20/20 in each eye without correction. (Waivers for defective visual acuity may be granted to a limited number of finalists.)

Each applicant is required to provide a medical history.

Applications for the NROTC program are available at your high school counseling office, U.S. Marine Corps recruiting stations and U.S. Navy recruiting districts.

Applicants for the NROTC scholarship program must have a social security number and must take either the SAT or the ACT at their own expense.

NROTC scholarships are awarded annually; therefore, it is a new program each year.

The Navy also has a two-year NROTC scholarship program that provides tuition, books, uniforms and $100 per month for the junior and senior years of college. This program is open to college sophomores. For information, write the Navy Opportunity Information Center, P.O. Box 2000, Pelham Manor, NY 10803.

Full information is also available from NROTC units at colleges and universities throughout the country:

University of California, Berkeley
University of California, Los Angeles
The Citadel, Charleston, South Carolina
University of Colorado, Boulder
Cornell University, Ithaca, New York
Duke University, Durham, North Carolina
University of Florida, Gainesville
Florida A & M. University, Tallahassee
Georgia Institute of Technology, Atlanta
College of the Holy Cross, Worcester, Massachusetts

University of Idaho, Moscow
University of Illinois, Champaign
Illinois Institute of Technology, Chicago
Iowa State University of Science and Technology, Ames
Jacksonville University, Jacksonville, Florida
University of Kansas, Lawrence
Maine Maritime Academy, Castine
Marquette University, Milwaukee, Wisconsin
Massachusetts Institute of Technology, Cambridge
Miami University, Oxford, Ohio
University of Michigan, Ann Arbor
University of Minnesota, Minneapolis
University of Mississippi, Mississippi State
University of Missouri, Columbia
University of Nebraska at Lincoln
University of North Carolina at Chapel Hill
Northwestern University, Evanston, Illinois
University of Notre Dame, Notre Dame, Indiana
Ohio State University, Columbus
University of Oklahoma, Norman
Oregon State University, Corvallis
University of Pennsylvania, Philadelphia
Pennsylvania State University, University Park
Prairie View A. & M. University, Prairie View, Texas
Purdue University, West LaFayette, Indiana
Rensselaer Polytechnic Institute, Troy, New York
William Marsh Rice University, Houston, Texas
University of Rochester, Rochester, New York
Savannah State College, Savannah, Georgia
University of South Carolina, Columbia
University of Southern California, Los Angeles
Southern University and A. & M. College, Baton Rouge,
    Louisiana
State University of New York Maritime College, Fort Schuyler,
    Bronx
Texas A. & M. University, College Station
University of Texas at Austin
Tulane University of Louisiana, New Orleans

University of Utah, Salt Lake City
Vanderbilt University, Nashville
Villanova University, Villanova, Pennsylvania
University of Virginia, Charlottesville
Virginia Military Institute, Lexington
University of Washington, Seattle
University of Wisconsin, Madison

For further information concerning the NROTC program, correspond directly with the commanding officer of the NROTC unit at one of the colleges and universities listed above.

The Air Force ROTC Program

Air Force Reserve Officers' Training Corps scholarships are available to qualified applicants in both four-year and two-year programs.

Each scholarship provides full tuition, laboratory and incidental fees and the full cost of required textbooks. In addition, scholarship cadets receive a tax-free $100 per month during the school year.

Four-year scholarships are available on a competitive basis to both men and women who are high school seniors or graduates and who enroll in certain scientific and engineering career fields, and to men who want to become Air Force pilots and navigators.

Students who wish to qualify for a four-year scholarship must complete a preliminary application process before December 15 of the year before the year they will enter college. College board examinations should be completed by the November testing cycle.

Applicant instruction bulletins may be obtained from your high school guidance counselor or by writing the AFROTC Advisory Service, Maxwell Air Force Base, Montgomery, AL 36112.

Other scholarship opportunities exist for students already in college. Four-year, three-year and two-year scholarships are available on a competitive basis. Applications for these scholarships should be made directly to the professor of aerospace studies at a college offering Air Force ROTC.

Men and women college freshmen engineering students who have at least four years of education remaining may compete for four-year scholarships.

Two-year scholarships are open to men who volunteer as missile launch officers and to men and women in nursing and selected pre-health professions curricula.

Three-year and two-year scholarships are awarded on the basis of collegiate grade point average, or ACT test results, academic major and potential active duty career field, a rating from an interview board composed of institutional officials and Air Force officers, scores on the rated portion of the Air Force Officer Qualifying Test and field training reports.

Students who apply for two-year scholarships in nursing or pre-health professions must also meet Professional Officer Course entrance requirements.

One Scholarship Leads to a Doctorate in a Health Career Field

Two-year Air Force ROTC pre-health professions scholarships are offered to encourage students to earn commissions through AFROTC and then to go on to acquire a doctorate in a health career field.

Additional tuition assistance for medical schooling expenses is guaranteed under the auspices of the Armed Forces Health Professions Scholarship Program for AFROTC pre-health professions scholarship graduates, upon acceptance to medical school.

This scholarship will sponsor an individual's remaining medical schooling, and those accepted into medical school will be transferred to the Medical Service Corps. This scholarship could be worth more than $60,000.

Who Is Eligible for an Air Force ROTC Scholarship?

Applicants for the AFROTC scholarship must be United States citizens or applicants for naturalization who are enrolled as full-time students at a college or university that offers or has a cross-enrollment agreement with Air Force ROTC.

Applicants must be in sound physical condition and have good moral character.

A recipient of an AFROTC four-year scholarship must be at least seventeen years of age and able to complete commissioning requirements without reaching twenty-five on June 30 of the year of commissioning.

A recipient who is not on scholarship status and not qualified for flying training should be able to complete commissioning requirements prior to age thirty.

General Qualifications for Admittance to the Professional Officer Course (POC)

Applicants for admittance to the Professional Officer Course (POC) must be at least seventeen years of age.

For the four-year program, they must complete the general military course and a four-week field training course; for the two-year program, they must complete the six-week field training course.

Applicants must attain current minimum score on the CEEB Scholastic Aptitude Test (SAT) or on the American College Test (ACT).

Selection is by a board of Air Force officers, and enlistment in the Air Force Reserve is required prior to entry into the Professional Officer Course.

Pre-health professions scholarship applicants must have a high grade-point average and certain academic prerequisites.

The Four-year Air Force ROTC Program

Students may pursue the four-year program on college campuses where it is in effect. Students enrolled in AFROTC (with the exception of scholarship recipients) may major in any field, but they cannot be commissioned until they have been awarded at least a bachelor's degree.

Enrollment procedures for the first two years of Air Force

ROTC (known as the General Military Course) are the same as for any college courses. GMC generally consists of one hour of classroom work and one hour of leadership laboratory each week.

Upon completion of the GMC requirements, cadets may compete for the last two years of the program, the Professional Officer Course (POC). The requirements for entry into the POC are listed above.

The Two-year Air Force ROTC Program

Applicants for the two-year program must have two years of studies, remaining at the undergraduate or the graduate level or a combination of the two.

Entry into the Professional Officer Course is highly competitive. Applicants must qualify using the same criteria as members of the GMC who are competing for POC entry.

Each applicant must successfully complete a six-week field training course at an Air Force base during the summer months. This course provides academic and military preparation for the competition for entry into the Professional Officer Course.

Cadets enrolled in the POC, and on scholarship, receive a tax-free allowance of $100 a month during the time of the course. Cadets on scholarship also receive paid tuition, laboratory fees, incidental expenses and textbooks.

Cadets and applicants receive pay, plus travel expenses for attendance at field training.

Cadets in the Flight Instruction Program receive free flying lessons from a civilian contractor near their campus.

All AFROTC uniforms and textbooks are provided by the Air Force both for on-campus courses and at field training.

Application for the two-year program should be made early in the academic year so that all requirements may be completed in time for assignment to summer field training.

Students interested in enrolling in the two-year program must contact the professor of aerospace studies at a campus where Air Force ROTC is offered.

College Scholarships for Enlistees in the Air Force

Enlisted members of the Air Force may apply for college scholarships through the Air Force ROTC Airmen Scholarship and Commissioning Program (AFROTC-ASCP).

This scholarship covers the cost of tuition, laboratory fees, books and other incidental fees, and it provides an allowance of $100 a month while the cadet is enrolled in aerospace studies courses and pursuing an academic curriculum leading to a degree and a second lieutenant's commission.

Air Force ROTC Medical Requirements

The medical requirements for admission to the Air Force ROTC are narrow and extensive. The requirements include:

At least 20/40 bilateral distant vision without glasses, correctable to 20/30 in one eye and 20/40 in the other.

Normal hearing.

Normal blood pressure.

Height between 64 and 80 inches for men and between 58 and 71 inches for women.

Normal weight for height and age.

No verified history of asthma since twelfth birthday.

No limiting physical infirmity.

Excellent dental health.

No history of disqualifying drug abuse.

There are further requirements for pilots and navigators (men only).

The Air Force ROTC has adopted an approach to learning that stresses student responsibility and involvement.

In classes conducted in small seminars, cadets engage in group discussions, debates, problem-solving and simulation activities that require maximum individual participation and group cooperation.

An essential part of this learning process is the expectation that students will evaluate critically what they read and what they say.

Colleges and Universities with Air Force ROTC Programs
or Cross-enrollment Agreements

Alabama
Auburn University, Auburn 36830
University of Alabama, University 35486
Samford University, Birmingham 35209
+Birmingham-Southern College, Birmingham 35204
+Jefferson State Jr College, Birmingham 35215 (GMC only)
+Lawson State Community College, Birmingham 35221 (GMC only)
+ Miles College, Birmingham 35208
+ University of Alabama, Birmingham, University Station 35294
+ University of Montevallo, Montevallo 35115
Tuskegee Institute, Tuskegee 36088
Troy State University, Troy 36081
Alabama State University, Montgomery 36101
+ Auburn University of Montgomery, Montgomery 36109
+ Huntingdon College, Montgomery 36106
+Troy State University at Montgomery, Montgomery 36104

Arizona
University of Arizona, Tucson 85721
+ Pima Community College, Tucson 85709 (GMC only)
Arizona State University, Tempe 85281
+ Glendale Community College, Glendale 85301 (GMC only)
+ Grand Canyon College, Phoenix 85017
+ Mesa Community College, Mesa 85222 (GMC only)
+ Phoenix College, Phoenix 85013 (GMC only)
+ Scottsdale Community College 85251 (GMC only)
Northern Arizona University, Flagstaff 86001

Arkansas
University of Arkansas, Fayetteville 72701

California
California State University, Fresno 93740
Loyola Marymount University, Los Angeles 90045

+ Schools having cross-enrollment agreements with AFROTC host universities. Schools designated "GMC Only" offer the first two years only of the Four-year AFROTC program. Consult the professor of aerospace studies at the AFROTC detachment on the university campus for enrollment procedures.
    * Four-year program only.
    ** Two-year program only.

+ California State University at Long Beach, Long Beach 90840
+ Cypress College, Cypress 90630 (GMC only)
+ East Los Angeles College, Los Angeles 90022 (GMC only)
+ El Camino College, El Camino 90506 (GMC only)
+ Fullerton College, Fullerton 92634 (GMC only)
+ Los Angeles City College, Los Angeles 90029 (GMC only)
+ Los Angeles Harbor College, Wilmington 90744 (GMC only)
+ Los Angeles Pierce College, Woodland Hills 91360 (GMC only)
+ Los Angeles SW College, Los Angeles 90047 (GMC only)
+ Los Angeles Trade Tech College, Los Angeles 90015 (GMC only)
+ Los Angeles Valley College, Van Nuys 91401 (GMC only)
+ Marymount Palos Verdes College, Palos Verdes Peninsula 90274
+ Mount St. Mary's College, Los Angeles 90049
+ Northrop University, Inglewood 90306
+ Santa Monica College, Santa Monica 90406 (GMC only)
+ West Los Angeles College, Culver City 90230 (GMC only)
San Jose State University, San Jose 95114
University of California, Los Angeles, Los Angeles 90024
University of Southern California, Los Angeles 90007
+ Biola College, La Mirada 90639
+ California Institute of Technology, Pasadena 91109
+ California Lutheran College, Thousand Oaks 91360
+ California State University at Fullerton, Fullerton 92631
+ California State University at Los Angeles, Los Angeles 90032
+ California State University at Long Beach, Long Beach 90801
+ California State University at Northridge, Los Angeles 91324
+ California State College, Dominguez Hills 90740
+ California State College, San Bernardino 92407
+ California State Polytechnic University, Pomona 91768
+ Chaffey College, Alta Loma 91701 (GMC only)
+ Chapman College, Orange 92666
+ Citrus College, Azusa 91702
+ Compton Community College, Compton 90221 (GMC only)
+ Cypress College, Cypress 90630 (GMC only)
+ East Los Angeles College, Los Angeles 90022 (GMC only)
+ El Camino College, El Camino 90506 (GMC only)
+ Fullerton College, Fullerton 92634 (GMC only)
+ Glendale Community College, Glendale 91208 (GMC only)
+ Golden West College, Huntington Beach 92647 (GMC only)
+ Hebrew Union College, Los Angeles 90007
+ Long Beach City College, Long Beach 90808 (GMC only)
+ Los Angeles City College, Los Angeles 90029 (GMC only)
+ Los Angeles Harbor College, Wilmington 90744 (GMC only)
+ Los Angeles Pierce College, Woodland Hills 91364 (GMC only)
+ Los Angeles SW College, Los Angeles 90047 (GMC only)

+ Los Angeles Trade and Technical College, Los Angeles 90015 (GMC only)
+ Los Angeles Valley College, Van Nuys 91401 (GMC only)
+ Moorpark College, Moorpark 93021 (GMC only)
+ Mt. San Antonio College, Walnut 91789 (GMC only)
+ Northrop University, Inglewood 90306
+ Occidental College, Los Angeles 90041
+ Orange Coast College, Costa Mesa 92626
+ Pasadena City College, Pasadena 91106 (GMC only)
+ Pepperdine University, Los Angeles 90044
+ Pepperdine University, Malibu 90265
+ Rio Hondo College, Whittier 90608
+ University of California, Irvine 92664
+ Ventura College, Ventura 93003 (GMC only)
+ West Los Angeles College, Culver City 90230 (GMC only)
+ Whittier College, Whittier 90608
San Diego State University, San Diego 92115
+ Point Loma College, San Diego 92106
San Francisco State University, San Francisco 94132
+ Golden Gate University, San Francisco 94106
+ University of California, Hastings College of Law, San Francisco 94102
+ Lone Mountain College, San Francisco 94118
+ University of California, San Francisco 94122
+ University of San Francisco, San Francisco 94117
University of California at Berkeley, Berkeley 94720
*California University at Hayward, Hayward 94540
*Contra Costa College, San Pablo 94806 (GMC only)
*Diablo Valley College, Pleasant Hill 94523

Colorado

Colorado State University, Fort Collins 80521
University of Northern Colorado, Greeley 80639
University of Colorado, Boulder 80302
*Metropolitan State College, Denver 80204
*Regis College, Denver 80221
*University of Colorado, Denver 80203
*University of Denver, Denver 80210

Connecticut

University of Connecticut, Storrs 06268
*Central Connecticut State College, New Britain 06050
*Eastern Connecticut State College, Willimantic 06226
u5District of Columbia
Howard University, Washington, D.C. 20059
*American University, Washington, D.C. 20016

*District of Columbia Teachers College, Washington, D.C. 20009
*Federal City College, Washington, D.C. 20005
*Gallaudet College, Washington, D.C. 20002
*Georgetown University, Washington, D.C. 20007
*George Washington University, Washington, D.C. 20006
*Catholic University of America, Washington, D.C. 20017
*Trinity College, Washington, D.C. 20017

Florida

Florida State University, Tallahassee 32306
*Florida A & M University, Tallahassee 32601
University of Florida, Gainesville 32601
University of Miami, P.O. Box 8164, Coral Gables 33124
*Barry College, Miami 33161
*Biscayne College, Miami 33054
*Florida International University, Miami 33144 (POC only)
*Miami-Dade Community College, North Campus, Miami 33157 (GMC only)
Miami-Dade Community College, South Campus, Miami 33156 (GMC only)
Embry-Riddle Aeronautical University, Daytona Beach 32015
Florida Technological University, Orlando 32816
*Lake-Sumter Community College, Leesburg 32748 (GMC only)
*Rollins College, Winter Park 32789
*Seminole Junior College, Sanford 32771 (GMC only)
*Valencia Community College, Orlando 32811 (GMC only)

Georgia

University of Georgia, Athens 30602
Georgia Institute of Technology, Atlanta 30332
*Clark College, Atlanta 30314
*Georgia State University, Atlanta 30303
*Morehouse College, Atlanta 30314
*Southern Technical Institute, Marietta 30060
Valdosta State College, Valdosta 31601

Hawaii

University of Hawaii, Honolulu 96822
*Chaminade College of Honolulu, Honolulu 96816

Illinois

University of Illinois, Urbana 61801
*Parkland College, Champaign 61820 (GMC only)
Illinois Institute of Technology, Chicago 60616
*Governors State University, Park Forest South 60466
*John Marshall Law School, Chicago 60604

*Kennedy-King College, Chicago 60621 (GMC only)
*Lewis University, Lockport 60441
*Loop College, Chicago 60601 (GMC only)
*Malcolm X College, Chicago 60612 (GMC only)
*Mayfair College, Chicago 60630 (GMC only)
*Northern Illinois University, DeKalb 60115
*Northeastern Illinois University, Chicago 60625
*Olive-Harvey College, Chicago 60028 (GMC only)
*Saint Xavier College, Chicago 60655
*Southwest College, Chicago 60652 (GMC only)
*Triton College, River Grove 60171 (GMC only)
*University of Illinois at Chicago Circle, Chicago 60680
*Wright College, Chicago 60634
Southern Illinois University at Carbondale, Carbondale 62901
Southern Illinois University at Edwardsville, Edwardsville 62025
*Belleville Area College, Belleville 62221 (GMC only)
*McKendree College, Lebanon 62254
Parks College of St. Louis University, Cahokia 62206

Indiana

Indiana University, Bloomington 47401
*Butler University, Indianapolis 46208
*DePauw University, Greencastle 46135
*Marian College, Indianapolis 46222
Purdue University, West Lafayette 47906
University of Notre Dame, Notre Dame 46556
*Holy Cross Junior College, Notre Dame 46556 (GMC only)
*Indiana University at South Bend, South Bend 46615
*St. Mary's College, Notre Dame 46556
University of Evansville, Evansville 47702
*Indiana State University of Evansville, Evansville 47712
*Indiana University, Southeast, New Albany, Indiana 47150

Iowa

Iowa State University, Ames 50010
*Des Moines Area Community College, Ankeny Campus, Ankeny 50021 (GMC only)
*Des Moines Area Community College, Boone 50036 (GMC only)
*Drake University, Des Moines 50311
*Grand View College, Des Moines 50416 (GMC only)
*Marshalltown Community College, Marshalltown 50158

University of Iowa, Iowa City 52242
*Iowa Western Community College, Council Bluffs 51501 (GMC only)

Kansas

Kansas State University, Manhattan 66506
Wichita State University, Wichita 67208
The University of Kansas, Lawrence 66045
Washburn University, Topeka 66621

Kentucky

University of Kentucky, Lexington 40506
*Georgetown College, Georgetown 40324
*Kentucky State University, Frankfort 40601
*Midway College, Midway 40347 (GMC only)
*Transylvania University, Lexington 40508
University of Louisville, Louisville 40208
*Bellarmine College, Louisville 40205
*Jefferson Community College, Louisville 40201 (GMC only)
*Louisville Presbyterian Theological Seminary, Louisville 40205
*Southern Baptist Theological Seminary, Louisville 40206
*Spalding College, Louisville 40203
*Northern Kentucky University, Highland Heights 41076
*Thomas More College, Fort Mitchell 41017

Louisiana

Louisiana Tech University, Ruston 71270
Louisiana State University and A & M College, Baton Rouge 70803
*Southern University and A & M College, Baton Rouge 70813
Grambling State University, Grambling 71245
University of Southwestern Louisiana, Lafayette 70501
Tulane University, New Orleans 70118
*Dillard University, New Orleans 70122
*Holy Cross College, New Orleans 70114
*Louisiana State University at New Orleans, New Orleans 70112
*Loyola University of New Orleans, New Orleans 70118
*Southern University in New Orleans, New Orleans 70126
*Xavier University of Louisiana, New Orleans 70125

Maryland

University of Maryland, College Park 20742
University of Maryland, Eastern Shore, Princess Anne 21853
*Salisbury State College, Salisbury 21801

Massachusetts

College of the Holy Cross, Worcester 01610
*Assumption College, Worcester 01609
*Anna Maria College, Paxton 01612
*Becker Junior College, Worcester 01609 (GMC only)
*Clark University, Worcester 01610
*Leicester Junior College, Leicester 01524 (GMC only)
*Quinsigamond Community College, Worcester 01606 (GMC only)
*Worcester Junior College, Worcester 01608 (GMC only)
*Worcester Polytechnic Institute, Worcester 01609
*Worcester State College, Worcester 01602
University of Lowell, Lowell 01854
*Bentley College, Waltham 02154
Massachusetts Institute of Technology, Cambridge 02139
*Northeastern University, Boston 02115
*Wellesley College, Wellesley 02181
University of Massachusetts, Amherst 01002

Michigan

Michigan State University, East Lansing 48821
*Lansing Community College, Lansing 48914 (GMC only)
University of Michigan, Ann Arbor 48104
*Eastern Michigan University, Ypsilanti 48197
*University of Michigan, Dearborn, Dearborn 48128
*Wayne State University, Detroit 48202
Michigan Technological University, Houghton 49931
*Suomi College, Hancock 49930 (GMC only)

Minnesota

College of St. Thomas, St. Paul 55105
*Anoka-Ramsey Community College, Coon Rapids 55433 (GMC only)
*Augsburg College, Minneapolis 55404
*College of St. Catherine, St. Paul 55105
*Hamline University, St. Paul 55104
*Inver Hills Community College, Inver Grove Heights 55057 (GMC only)
*Lakewood Community College, White Bear Lake 55110 (GMC only)
*Macalester College, St. Paul 55106
*North Hennepin Community College, Brooklyn Park 55445
University of Minnesota, Minneapolis 55455
University of Minnesota at Duluth, Duluth 55812
*College of St. Scholastica, Duluth 55811
*Concordia College, Moorhead 56560
*Moorhead State University, Moorhead 56560

Mississippi

Mississippi State University, State College 39762
University of Mississippi, University 38677
University of Southern Mississippi, Hattiesburg 39401
*William Carey College, Hattiesburg 39401
Mississippi Valley State University, Itta Bena 38941

Missouri

Southeast Missouri State University, Cape Girardeau 63701
University of Missouri, Columbia 65201
*Columbia College, Columbia 65201
*Harris-Stowe College, St. Louis, Missouri 63103
*St. Louis University, St. Louis, Missouri 63108
*University of Missouri at St. Louis, Missouri 63121
*Washington University, St. Louis, Missouri 63130

Montana

Montana State University, Bozeman 59715

Nebraska

University of Nebraska, Lincoln 68588
*Concordia Teachers College, Seward 68434
*Nebraska Wesleyan University, Lincoln 68504
University of Nebraska at Omaha, Omaha 68101
*Creighton University, Omaha 68178

New Hampshire

University of New Hampshire, Durham 03824

New Jersey

Rutgers, The State University, New Brunswick 08903
*Brookdale Community College, Lincroft 07738 (GMC only)
*Mercer County Community College, Trenton 08690 (GMC only)
*Middlesex County College, Edison 08817 (GMC only)
*Monmouth College, West Long Branch 07764
*Rider College, Trenton 08602
*Somerset County College, Somerville 08876 (GMC only)
*Trenton State College, Trenton 08625
*Union College, Cranford 07016 (GMC only)
New Jersey Institute of Technology, Newark 07102
*Kean College of New Jersey, Union 07083
*Montclair State College, Upper Montclair 07043
*William Paterson College, Wayne 07470
Stevens Institute of Technology, Hoboken 07030

   *Jersey City State College, Jersey City 07305
   *St. Peter's College, Jersey City 07306

New Mexico
   New Mexico State University, Las Cruces 88003
   University of New Mexico, Albuquerque 87131
   *University of Albuquerque 87120

New York
   Cornell University, Ithaca 14853
   *Corning Community College, Corning 14830 (GMC only)
   *Eisenhower College, Seneca Falls 13148
   *Ithaca College, Ithaca 14850
   *SUNY at Binghamton, Binghamton 13901
   *SUNY at Cortland, Cortland 13045
   *Tompkins-Cortland Community College, Dryden 13053 (GMC only)
   Syracuse University, Syracuse 13210
   *Le Moyne College, Syracuse 13214
   *SUNY, College of Environmental Science and Forestry, Syracuse 13210
   *Utica College of Syracuse University, Utica 13502
   Rensselaer Polytechnic Institute, Troy 13181
   *Albany College of Pharmacy, Albany 12208
   *College of St. Rose, Albany 12203
   *SUNY Empire State College, Saratoga Springs 12866
   *Fulton-Montgomery Community College, Johnstown 12095 (GMC only)
   *Hudson Valley Community College, Troy 12180 (GMC only)
   *Immaculate Conception Seminary, Troy 12180
   *Junior College of Albany, Albany 12208 (GMC only)
   *Russell Sage College, Troy 12180
   *Schenectady County Community College, Schenectady 12305 (GMC only)
   **Siena College, Loudonville 12211
   *Skidmore College, Saratoga Springs 12866
   *State University of New York, Albany 12210
   *Union College, Schenectady 12308
   Manhattan College, Bronx 10471
   *College of Mount St. Vincent, Riverdale 10471

North Carolina
   Duke University, Durham 27706
   *North Carolina Central University, Durham 27707
   University of North Carolina at Chapel Hill 27514
   North Carolina State University at Raleigh, Raleigh 27607
   *Meredith College, Raleigh 27611
   *Peace College, Raleigh 27602 (GMC only)

*St. Augustine's College, Raleigh 27611
*St. Mary's College, Raleigh 27611 (GMC only)
*Shaw University, Raleigh 27602
East Carolina University, Greenville 27834
*Pitt Technical Institute, Greenville 27834 (GMC only)
North Carolina A & T State University, Greensboro 27411
*Bennett College, Greensboro 27420
*Greensboro College, Greensboro 27420
*Guilford College, Greensboro 27310
*High Point College, High Point 27262
*University of North Carolina at Greensboro 27412
Fayetteville State University, Fayetteville 28301

North Dakota
North Dakota State University, Fargo 58102
University of North Dakota, Grand Forks 58202

Ohio
Bowling Green State University, Bowling Green 43403
*Bowling Green State University; Firelands Campus, Huron 44839 (GMC only)
*University of Toledo, Toledo 43606
Kent State University, Kent 44242
*Cleveland State University, Cleveland 44115
Miami University, Oxford 45056
Ohio State University, Columbus 43210
*Ohio Wesleyan University, Delaware 43115
*Otterbein College, Westerville 43081
Capital University, Columbus 43209
*Columbus Technical Institute, Columbus 43215 (GMC only)
*Ohio Dominican College, Columbus 43219
Ohio University, Athens 45701
University of Akron, Akron 44325
University of Cincinnati, Cincinnati 45221
*Edgecliff College, Cincinnati 45206
*Xavier University, Cincinnati 45007

Oklahoma
Oklahoma State University, Stillwater 74074
University of Oklahoma, Norman 73069

Oregon
Oregon State University, Corvallis 97331
University of Oregon, Eugene 97403

*Northwest Christian College, Eugene 97401
University of Portland 97203
*Clackamas Community College, Oregon City 97045 (GMC only)
*Concordia College, Portland 97211 (GMC only)
*Mount Hood Community College, Gresham 97030 (GMC only)
*Portland Community College, Portland 97219 (GMC only)
*Portland State University, Portland 97207

Pennsylvania
Lehigh University, Bethlehem 18015
*Allentown College of St. Francis de Sales, Center Valley 18034
*Cedar Crest College, Allentown, 18104
*Lafayette College, Easton 18042
*Moravian College, Bethlehem 18018
*Muhlenberg College, Allentown 18104
*Northampton County Area Community College, Bethlehem 18017 (GMC only)
Pennsylvania State University: Allentown, Allentown 18051 (GMC only)
Pennsylvania State University, University Park 16802
University of Pittsburgh, Pittsburgh 15260
*Carlow College, Pittsburgh 15213
*Carnegie-Mellon University, Pittsburgh 15213
*Chatham College, Pittsburgh 15232
*Community College of Allegheny County, Pittsburgh 15219 (GMC only)
*Duquesne University, Pittsburgh 15219
*Point Park College, Pittsburgh 15222
*Robert Morris College, Coraopolis 15108
Grove City College, Grove City 16127
*Slippery Rock State College, Slippery Rock 16057
Wilkes College, Wilkes-Barre 18703
*Bloomsburg State College, Bloomsburg 17815
*Keystone Junior College, La Plume 18440 (GMC only)
*King's College, Wilkes-Barre 18711
*Lackawanna Junior College, Scranton 18503 (GMC only)
*Luzerne County Community College, Wilkes-Barre 18711 (GMC only)
*Marywood College, Scranton 18509
*Misericordia College, Dallas 18612
*Pennsylvania State University: Hazelton Campus, Hazelton 18201 (GMC only)
*Pennsylvania State University: Wilkes-Barre Campus, Wilkes-Barre 18708 (GMC only)
*Pennsylvania State University: Worthington-Scranton Campus, Dunmore 18512 (GMC only)
*University of Scranton, Scranton 18510

Puerto Rico

University of Puerto Rico, Rio Piedras 00936
*Bayamon Central University, Bayamon 00619
*Inter American University of Puerto Rico: San Juan 00936
*Inter American University of Puerto Rico: Bayamon 00619
*University of Puerto Rico: Bayamon Regional College, Bayamon 00619
*University of Puerto Rico: Carolina Regional College, Carolina 00630 (GMC only)
University of Puerto Rico: Mayaguez Campus, Mayaguez 00708
*University of Puerto Rico: Aguadilla Regional College, Aguadilla 00603
*Inter American University of Puerto Rico, San German 00753

South Carolina

The Citadel, Charleston 29409
Clemson University, Clemson 29631
*Anderson College, Anderson 29621 (GMC only)
*Central Wesleyan College, Central 29630
Baptist College at Charleston, Charleston 29411
University of South Carolina, Columbia 29208
*Benedict College, Columbia 29204
Newberry College, Newberry 29108

Texas

*University of Texas at El Paso, El Paso 79968

Washington

*Clark College, Vancouver 98663 (GMC only)

16

The Granddaddy of Federal Financial Aid— The GI Bill

This was the historical beginning of federal financial aid assistance.

GI Bill Educational Training provides for veterans of the post-Korean conflict period and the Vietnam era and service personnel.

Veterans who served on active duty for more than 180 continuous days (part of which must have occurred after January 31, 1955, but before January 1, 1977) and who were released under conditions other than dishonorable, discharged for a service-connected disability or continue on active duty are eligible under the Veterans Readjustment Benefits Act of 1966, as amended.

Those individuals are also eligible who contracted with the armed forces and were enlisted in or assigned to a Reserve unit prior to January 1, 1977, and who, as a result of this enlistment or assignment, served on active duty for more than 180 days, any part of which began within twelve months after January 1, 1977.

Veterans must have been discharged from active duty under conditions other than dishonorable.

The 181-day active duty requirement does not include any period of full-time assignment by the armed forces to a civilian institution for a course substantially the same as one offered to civilians or any period of service as a cadet or midshipman at a service academy.

If a veteran has served in the Reserve or the National Guard (but not at one of the service academies) and later serves at least one consecutive year on active duty, the active duty for training time initially served shall be treated as active duty for veterans' education purposes.

What Educational Institutions Can Veterans Attend?

Veterans can attend any educational institution approved for training, including any public or private school, elementary or high school, vocational, correspondence or business school, junior or teachers' college, normal school, college or university, professional, scientific or technical institution or any other institution that furnishes education at the secondary school level or above.

Veterans who have already qualified in a program of education may receive educational assistance for up to six months to pursue refresher training to update skills acquired prior to or during service.

Eligible veterans may select a program of training at any educational institution or training establishment that will accept and retain the individual as a student in any field or branch of knowledge which the institution finds the person qualified to undertake.

Educational and vocational counseling will be provided by the Veterans Administration upon request.

What Is the Period of Eligibility?

Each eligible person (one who entered service before January 1, 1977, or, in some cases, after that date) will be entitled to educational assistance for a period of one and one-half months for each month or fraction thereof of service on active duty after January 31, 1955, up to a total of forty-five months.

Those persons are also entitled to forty-five months who, pursuant to a contract with the armed forces, entered prior to January 1, 1977, served eighteen continuous months or more on active duty, their service having begun between January 1, 1977, and January 1, 1978, and who are discharged or released from such active duty under conditions other than dishonorable.

Veterans who began their service before January 1, 1977 (or in some cases after that date in the Delayed Entry Program or similar program), and who are released from active duty after January 31, 1955, have eligibility for ten years after discharge or release, but only until December 31, 1989.

Veterans who were prevented from beginning or completing their chosen program of education because of a physical or mental disability not the result of their own willful misconduct may receive an extension of delimiting date. The following table shows the monthly allowance for living expenses under the GI Bill.

Educational Course Loan	No Dependents	One Dependent	Two Dependents	Each Additional Dependent
Full time	$311	$370	$422	$26
Three-fourths time	233	277	317	19
Half-time	156	185	211	13

Application forms are available at all VA offices, active-duty stations and American embassies. When completed, forms should be submitted to the nearest VA office or American embassy.

Vocational Rehabilitation for Disabled Veterans

Veterans who served in the armed forces during World War II or thereafter are eligible for vocational rehabilitation if all three of the following conditions are met:

1. They suffered a service-connected disability in active service that entitles them to compensation (or would do so but for receipt of retirement pay).

2. They were discharged or released under other than dishonorable conditions.

3. The VA determines that they need vocational rehabilitation to overcome the handicap of their disabilities.

Generally, a veteran is eligible for vocational rehabilitation for nine years following discharge or release. A further extension may be granted veterans who are seriously disabled when the VA determines that this is necessary because of the veteran's disability and need for vocational rehabilitation.

Eligible disabled veterans may get training up to a total of four years or the equivalent in part-time or a combination of part-time and full-time training, which in some cases may exceed four years.

Before a disabled veteran begins training, he or she will be provided vocational counseling to assist in the selection of a suitable occupation and in the development of a vocational rehabilitation plan.

Eligible veterans have several options; they may enroll in schools or colleges, train on the job, take institutional on-farm training, enter programs that combine school and job training or train in special rehabilitation facilities or at home (when necessary because of serious disability).

Subsistence Allowance

While in training and for two months after rehabilitation, eligible disabled veterans may receive subsistence allowances *in addition to* their disability compensation. The costs of tuition, books and fees are paid by the VA.

The following table shows the monthly allowance for living expenses for veterans enrolled in a vocational rehabilitation program:

Educational Course Loan	No Dependents	One Dependent	Two Dependents	Each Additional Dependent
Full time	$241	$298	$351	$26
Three-fourths time	181	224	263	19
Half-time	120	149	176	13

Veterans may apply at any VA office.

Survivors' and Dependents' Education

Survivors of deceased veterans, spouses of living veterans and children of either between the ages of eighteen and twenty-six are eligible when the death or permanent and total disability was the result of service in the armed forces after the beginning of the Spanish-American War on April 28, 1898.

If eligible children under eighteen have graduated from high school or are above the age of compulsory school attendance, the VA may begin this schooling before they reach age eighteen.

In some instances, handicapped children may begin a special vocational or restoration course as early as age fourteen.

The period of eligibility for educational assistance or special restorative training ends on a child's twenty-sixth birthday (unless extended in special conditions).

A child's marriage will be no barrier to eligibility; a surviving spouse's remarriage terminates entitlement unless the remarriage is ended by death or divorce.

Monthly allowances are $300 in full-time programs, $233 in three-fourths time programs and $156 in half-time programs.

Allowances for programs of less than half time are limited to tuition cost, not to exceed $156. The allowance for programs of one-fourth time or less is $78.

Those enrolled full time in cooperative courses—alternating classroom study and related experience on the job—will receive $251 per month.

Survivors and dependents may apply at any VA office.

17

If You Are a Veteran, the VA Has a Program for You

Veterans enrolled full time in a college degree, vocational or professional program under the GI Bill, or in a vocational rehabilitation program (Title 38, United States Code), are eligible to earn as they learn in the VA work-study program.

Preference in selection will be given to those who have a service-connected disability of 30 percent or more.

The number of applicants selected will depend on the availability of VA-related work at schools or VA facilities in each area.

Veterans in the program may work a maximum of 250 hours per semester (or other enrollment periods), and they will be paid the minimum hourly wage or $2.65 an hour, whichever is greater. Veterans may work less than 250 hours, depending on work availability and individual schedules.

If you are interested in this program, you should see the veterans' representative on your campus or your financial aid officer, or contact the Veterans' Services Division of the VA regional office serving your area. You will find a toll-free telephone number for the Veterans Administration in your telephone book.

Educational Assistance for Disabled Veterans

If you are a disabled veteran, you can get VA financial assistance in obtaining a college or university education.

The VA will also give financial assistance to disabled veterans who attend trade schools, business schools or technical schools.

You are eligible for this assistance if you are a veteran who

161

has a disability of compensable degree as a result of active service during World War II or thereafter and if you have been or will be discharged, released or retired from service under other than dishonorable conditions.

The Veterans Administration will determine whether you need training to overcome the handicapping effect of your service-connected disability.

In order to participate, your period of eligibility must not have expired. You have nine years from the date of your discharge to complete your training; however, if you have been separated from the armed forces for a longer period, you may still be eligible if certain conditions prevented you from training, or if you are found to be seriously disabled.

The VA will pay your training expenses, including tuition, fees, necessary books, supplies and equipment, and will provide you with a monthly subsistence allowance while you are in training. This is in addition to any compensation or other benefits to which you are entitled.

The kinds of training available under this program are college or university education; trade school, business school or technical school education; apprenticeship or other on-the-job training; on-farm training; training in a rehabilitation facility, a sheltered workshop or in your own home (if your disability requires it); or a combination of these kinds of training.

To apply write the nearest VA office or center. If you are hospitalized and awaiting disability discharge, send your application, VA Form 22-1900, and your medical records to the nearest VA office or center.

For information or assistance in applying for veterans' benefits, write, call, or visit a Veterans Benefits Counselor at your nearest VA regional office or VA office listed below, or a local veterans service organization representative. Application for medical benefits may be made at a VA hospital or any VA station with medical facilities.

All 50 states have toll-free telephone services to VA regional offices. The telephone numbers listed after each regional office are the toll-free benefits information numbers to that office for the areas shown. Local telephone numbers are also listed for VA hospitals and clinics.

Please note: Telephone numbers are subject to change. If you are unable to reach VA at the number listed for your area or if you are unsure which number to call, consult the white pages of your local telephone directory under U.S. Government, Veterans Administration, for the benefits information number. The directory assistance operator can also assist you.

GI life insurance is administered at the VA Center in St. Paul or Philadelphia. For any information concerning a policy, write directly to the VA Center administering it, give the insured's policy number, if known. The insured's full name, date of birth, and service number should be given if the policy number is not known.

VA INSTALLATIONS—WHERE TO GO FOR HELP

VA installations are listed below by state. Information on VA benefits may be obtained from the following installations: Regional Offices (RO); other offices (O); Centers (C) (Regional Offices and Insurance); and United States Veterans Assistance Centers (USVAC) listed immediately following the state listing below. Abbreviations of other installations are as follows: H—Hospitals; D—Domiciliary; NHC—Nursing Home Care; OC—Outpatient Clinic (independent); OCH—Outpatient Clinic (physically separated from hospital); OCS—Outpatient Clinic Substation.

Alabama
Birmimgham (H) 35233
    700 S. 19th St.
    (205) 933–8101
Mobile (OCS) 36617
    2451 Fillingim St.
    (205) 690–2875
Montgomery (H) 36109
    215 Perry Hill Rd.
    (205) 272–4670
Montgomery (RO) 36104
    474 S. Court St.
If you reside in the local telephone area of:
    Birmingham—322–2492
    Huntsville—539–7742

Alabama *(continued)*
>   Mobile—432–8645
>   Montgomery—832–7581
> All other areas in Alabama
>   (800) 392–8054
> Tuscaloosa (H&NHC) 35401
>   Loop Rd.
>   (205) 553–3760
> Tuskegee (H&NHC) 36083
>   (205) 727–0550

Alaska
> Anchorage (O) 99501
>   Rm. 214, Loussac-Sogn Bldg.
>   429 D St.
>   Zenith 2500
> Juneau (RO) 99802
>   Federal Bldg., U.S. Post Office and Courthouse
>   709 W. 9th St.
> If you live in the local telephone area of:
>   Anchorage—276–5143
>   Juneau—586–7472
> All other Alaska communities ask operator for Zenith 2500
> Juneau (OC) 99802
>   Federal Bldg., U.S. Post Office and Courthouse
>   709 W. 9th St.
>   (907) 586–7466

Arizona
> Phoenix (H) 85012
>   7th St. & Indian School Rd.
>   (602) 277–5551
> Phoenix (RO) 85012
>   3225 N. Central Ave.
> If you live in the local telephone area of:
>   Phoenix—263–5411
>   Tucson—622–6424
> All other Arizona areas (800) 352–0451
> Prescott (H&D) 86313
>   (602) 445–4860
> Tucson (H&NHC) 85723
>   3601 S. 6th Ave.
>   (602) 792–1450

Arkansas

Fayetteville (H) 72701
1100 N. College Ave.
(501) 443-2301
Little Rock (RO) 72201
1200 W. 3rd St.
If you live in the local telephone area of:
Fort Smith—785-2637
Little Rock—378-5971
Pine Bluff—536-8100
Texarkana—774-2166
All other Arkansas areas (800) 482-8990
Little Rock (H&NHC) 72206
300 E. Roosevelt Rd.
(501) 372-8361

California

Compton (USVAC) 90221
1717 N. Long Beach Blvd.
Suite 108
(213) 537-3203
East Los Angeles (USVAC) 90063
East L.A. Service Center
929 N. Bonnie Beach Pl.
(213) 264-1068
Fresno (H) 93703
2615 E. Clinton Ave.
(209) 227-2941
Livermore (H) 94550
(415) 447-2560
Loma Linda (H) 92354
11201 Benton St.
(714) 824-0850
Long Beach (H&NHC) 90822
5901 E. 7th St.
(213) 498-1313
Los Angeles (USVAC)
Federal Building
11000 Wilshire Blvd.
West Los Angeles
824-7479
Los Angeles (RO) 90024
Federal Building

California *(continued)*
>   11000 Wilshire Blvd.
>   West Los Angeles
>
> Counties of Inyo, Kern, Los Angeles, Orange, San Bernardino, San Luis Obispo, Santa Barbara and Ventura:
> If you live in the local telephone area of:
>   Central LA—879-1303
>   Inglewood—645-5420
>   La Crescenta—248-0450
>   Malibu—451-0672
>   San Fernando—997-6401
>   San Pedro—833-5241
>   Sierra Madre—355-3305
>   West Los Angeles—479-4011
>   Whittier—945-3841
> Outside LA
>   Anaheim—821-1020
>   Bakersfield—834-3142
>   Huntington Beach—848-1500
>   Ontario—983-9784
>   Oxnard—487-3977
>   San Bernardino—884-4874
>   Santa Ana—543-8403
>   Santa Barbara—963-0643
> All other areas of the above counties—(800) 352-6592
> Counties of Alpine, Lassen, Modoc and Mono served by:
> Reno, NV (RO) 89520
>   1201 Terminal Way
> If you live in the above California counties—
>   (800) 648-5406
> Los Angeles (H&D) 90073
>   Sawtelle & Wilshire Blvd.
>   (213) 478-3711
> Los Angeles (OC) 90013
>   425 S. Hill St.
>   (213) 688-2000
> Martinez (H) 94553
>   150 Muir Rd.
>   (415) 228-6800
> Oakland (OCS) 94612
>   1515 Clay St.
>   (415) 273-7125
> Palo Alto (H&NHC) 94304
>   3801 Miranda Ave.
>   (415) 493-5000

California *(continued)*
    San Diego (RO) 92108
      2022 Camino Del Rio North
    Counties of Imperial, Riverside, and San Diego:
    If you live in the local telephone area of:
      Riverside—686–1132
      San Diego—297–8220
    All other areas of the above counties (800) 532–3811
    San Diego (H&NHC) 92161
      3350 LaJolla Village Dr.
      (714) 453–7500
    San Diego (OCH) 92108
      Palomar Building
      2022 Camino Del Rio North
    San Francisco (RO) 94105
      211 Main St.
    If you live in the local telephone area of:
      Fremont—796–9212
      Fresno—(800) 652–1296
      Modesto—521–9260
      Monterey—649–3550
      Oakland—893–0405
      Palo Alto—321–5615
      Sacramento—929–5863
      San Francisco—495–8900
      San Jose—998–7373
      Santa Rosa—544–3520
      Stockton—948–8860
      Vallejo—552–1556
    All other areas of Northern California
      (800) 652–1240
    San Francisco (H) 94121
      4150 Clement St.
      (415) 221–4810
    Sepulveda (H&NHC) 91343
      16111 Plummer
      (213) 894–8271

Colorado
    Denver (RO) 80225
      Building 20
      Denver Federal Center
    If you live in the local telephone area of:
      Colorado Springs—475–9911

Colorado *(continued)*
    Denver—233–6300
    Pueblo—545–1764
All other Colorado areas—
    (800) 332–6742
Denver (H) 80220
    1055 Clermont St.
    (303) 399–8020
Fort Lyon (H&NHC) 81038
    (303) 456–1260
Grand Junction (H&NHC) 81501
    2121 North Ave.
    (303) 242–0731

Connecticut
    Hartford (RO) 06103
    450 Main St.
If you live in the local telephone area of:
    Bridgeport—384–9861
    Danbury—743–2791
    Hartford—278–3230
    New Haven—562–2113
    New London—447–0377
    Norwalk—853–8141
    Stamford—325–4039
    Waterbury—757–0347
All other Connecticut areas—
    (800) 842–4315
Newington (H) 06111
    555 Willard Ave.
    (203) 666–4361
West Haven (H&NHC) 06516
    W. Spring St.
    (203) 933–2561

Delaware
    Wilmington (RO) 19805
    1601 Kirkwood Highway
If you live in the local telephone area of:
    Wilmington—998–0191
All other Delaware areas—
    (800) 292–7855
Wilmington (H) 19805
    1601 Kirkwood Highway
    (302) 994–2511

District of Columbia
Washington, D.C. (RO) 20421
941 N. Capitol St., N.E.
(202) 872–1151
Washington, D.C. (H) 20422
50 Irving St., N.W.
(202) 483–6666

Florida
Bay Pines (H, D, NHC, & OCH) 33504
1000 Bay Pines Blvd., N.
(813) 391–9644
Gainesville (H) 32602
Archer Rd.
(904) 376–1611
Jacksonville (O) 32201
Post Office & Courthouse Bldg.
311 W. Monroe St.
(904) 946–3657
Jacksonville (OCS) 32201
311 W. Monroe St.
(904) 791–2751
Lake City (H&NHC) 32055
S. Marion St.
(904) 752–1400
Miami (H&NHC) 33125
1201 N.W. 16th St.
(305) 324–4455
Miami (O) 33130
Federal Building, Rm. 100
51 S.W. 1st Ave.
(305) 358–0669
Orlando (OCS) 32806
83 W. Columbia St.
(305) 425–7521
Riviera Beach (OPC) 33404
Exec. Plaza, 301 Broadway
(305) 845–2800
St. Petersburg (OHC) 33731
144 1st Ave. S.
(813) 893–3526
St. Petersburg (RO) 33731
144 1st Ave. S.

Florida *(continued)*

If you live in the local telephone area of:

Cocoa/Cocoa Beach—783–8930

Daytona Beach—255–8351

Ft. Lauderdale/Hollywood—522–4725

Ft. Myers—344–0900

Gainesville—376–5266

Jacksonville—356–1581

Lakeland/Winter Haven—683–7481

Melbourne—724–5600

Miami—358–0669

Orlando—425–2626

Pensacola—434–3537

Sarasota—366–2939

Tallahassee—224–6872

Tampa—229–0451

West Palm Beach—833–5734

St. Petersburg—898–2121

All other Florida areas—

(800) 282–8821

Tampa (H) 33612

13000 N. 30th St.

(813) 971–4500

Georgia

Atlanta (RO) 30308

730 Peachtree St., N.E.

If you live in the local telephone area of:

Albany—439–2331

Athens—549–8893

Atlanta—881–1776

Augusta—738–5403

Columbus—324–6646

Macon—745–6517

Savannah—232–3365

All other Georgia areas—

(800) 282–0232

Augusta (H&NHC) 30904

(404) 733–4471

Decatur (H) 30033

1670 Clairmont Rd., N.E.

(404) 321–6111

Dublin (H, D & NHC) 31021

(912) 272–1210

Hawaii

Honolulu (RO) 96850
PJKK Federal Bldg.
300 Ala Moana Blvd.
If you live in the local telephone area of:
Is. of Hawaii—Ask operator for Enterprise 5308
Is. of Kauai—Ask operator for Enterprise 5310
Is. of Maui/Lanai/Molokai—Ask operator for Enterprise 5309
Is. of Oahu—546–8962
Honolulu Clinic 96801
P.O. Box 3198
680 Ala Moana Blvd.
(808) 546–2176

Idaho

Boise (RO) 83724
Federal Bldg. and U.S. Courthouse
550 W. Fort St.
If you live in the local telephone area of:
Boise—345–7491
All other Idaho areas—
(800) 632–2003
Boise (H) 83702
5th and Fort St.
(208) 342–3681

Illinois

Chicago (H) 60611
333 E. Huron St. (Lakeside)
(312) 943–6600
Chicago (H) 60680
(West Side)
820 S. Damen Ave.
(312) 666–6500
Chicago (RO) 60611
536 S. Clark St.
If you live in the local telephone area of:
Bloomington/Normal—829–4374
Carbondale—457–8161
Champaign-Urbana—344–7505
Chicago—663–5510
Decatur—429–9445

Illinois *(continued)*

 E. St. Louis—274–5444
 Peoria—674–0901
 Rockford—968–0538
 Springfield—789–1246
 All other Illinois areas—
  (800) 972–5327
 Danville (H&NHC) 61832
  (217) 442–8000
 Hines (H) 60141
  (312) 343–7200
 Marion (H) 62959
  (618) 993–3236
 North Chicago (H&NHC) 60064
  Downey
  (312) 689–1900

Indiana

 Evansville (OCS) 47708
  214 S.E. 6th St.
  (812) 423–6871 Ext. 316
 Fort Wayne (H&NHC) 46805
  1600 Randalia Dr.
  (219) 743–5431
 Indianapolis (RO) 46204
  575 N. Pennsylvania St.
 If you live in the local telephone area of:
  Anderson/Muncie—289–9377
  Evansville—426–1403
  Ft. Wayne—422–9189
  Gary/Hammond/E. Chicago—886–9184
  Indianapolis—635–5221
  Lafayette/W. Lafayette—742–0084
  South Bend—232–3011
  Terre Haute—232–1030
 All other Indiana areas—
  (800) 382–4540
 Indianapolis (H&NHC) 46202
  1481 W. 10th St.
  (317) 635–7401
 Marion (H&NHC) 46952
  E. 38th St.
  (317) 674–3321

Iowa

Des Moines (RO) 50309
210 Walnut St.
If you live in the local telephone area of:
Cedar Rapids—366–7681
Davenport/Rock Is./Moline, IL—326–4051
Des Moines—280–7220
Sioux City—252–3291
Waterloo—235–6721
All other areas—
(800) 362–2222
Des Moines (H) 50310
30th & Euclid Ave.
(515) 255–2173
Iowa City (H) 52240
(319) 338–0581
Knoxville (H&NHC) 50138
1515 W. Pleasant St.
(515) 842–3101

Kansas

Leavenworth (H, D & NHC) 66048
4201 S. 4th St., Trafficway
(913) 682–2000
Topeka (H&NHC) 66622
2200 Gage Blvd.
(913) 272–3111
Wichita (RO) 67218
5500 E. Kellogg
If you live in the local telephone area of:
Kansas City—432–1650
Topeka—357–5301
Wichita—685–2221
All other areas—
(800) 362–3353
Wichita (H) 67218
5500 E. Kellogg
(316) 685–2221

Kentucky

Lexington (H&NHC) 40507
(606) 233–4511

Kentucky *(continued)*
Louisville (RO) 40202
600 Federal Place
If you live in the local telephone area of:
Lexington—253–0566
Louisville—584–2231
All other areas—(800) 292–4562
Louisville (H) 40202
800 Zorn Ave.
(502) 895–3401

Louisiana
Alexandria (H&NHC) 71301
(318) 442–0251
New Orleans (RO) 70113
701 Loyola Ave.
If you live in the local telephone area of:
Baton Rouge—343–5539
New Orleans—561–0121
Shreveport—424–8442
All other Louisiana areas—
(800) 462–9510
New Orleans (H) 70146
1601 Perdido St.
(504) 524–0811
Shreveport (H&O) 71130
510 E. Stoner Ave.
(318) 221–8411 (Office)
(318) 423–8411 (Hospital)

Maine
Portland (O) 04111
One Maine Savings Plaza
Congress St.
775–6391
Togus (RO) 04330
If you live in the local telephone area of:
Portland—775–6391
Togus—623–8411
All other Maine areas—
(800) 452–1935
Togus (H&NHC) 04330
(207) 623–8411

Maryland

Counties of Montgomery and Prince Georges:
Washington, DC (RO) 20421
  941 N. Capitol St., N.E.
If you live in the above Maryland counties—872–1151
All other Maryland Counties:
  Baltimore (RO) 21201
  31 Hopkins Plaza
  Federal Building
If you live in the local telephone area of:
  Baltimore—685–5454
All other Maryland areas:
  (800) 492–9503
Baltimore (OCH) 21201
  31 Hopkins Plaza
  Federal Building
  (301) 962–4610
Baltimore (H) 21218
  3900 Loch Raven Blvd.
  (301) 467–9932
Fort Howard (H&NHC) 21052
  (301) 477–1800
Perry Point (H&NHC) 21902
  (301) 962–4725

Massachusetts

Bedford (H&NHC) 01730
  200 Spring Rd.
  (617) 275–7500
Boston (H) 02130
  150 S. Huntington Ave.
  (617) 232–9500
Towns of Fall River and New Bedford and counties of Barnstable, Dukes,
  Nantucket, part of Plymouth, and Bristol are served by
Providence, R.I. (RO) 02903
  321 S. Main St.
If you live in the local telephone area of:
  Fall River—676–3898
  New Bedford—999–1321
All other areas of Dukes, Nantucket, Barnstable, and parts of Plymouth,
and Bristol counties—
  (800) 556–3893
Remaining Massachusetts counties served by:

Massachusetts *(continued)*
  Boston (RO) 02203
    John Fitzgerald Kennedy Federal Bldg.
    Government Center
  If you live in the local telephone area of:
    Boston—227–4600
    Brockton—588–0764
    Fitchburg/Leominster—342–8927
    Haverhill—374–4721
    Lawrence—687–3332
    Lowell—445–5463
    Pittsfield—499–2890
    Springfield—785–5343
    Worcester—791–3595
  All other Massachusetts areas—
    (800) 392–6015
  Boston (OC) 02108
    17 Court St.
    (617) 223–2020
  Brockton (H&NHC) 02401
    945 Belmont St.
    (617) 583–4500
  Lowell (OCS) 01852
    Old Post Office Bldg.
    50 Kearney Square
    (617) 453–1746
  New Bedford (OCS) 02740
    53 N. Sixth St.
    (617) 997–8721
  Northampton (H&NHC) 01060
    N. Main St.
    (413) 584–4040
  Springfield (O) 01103
    1200 Main St.
    (413) 785–5343
  Springfield (OCS) 01103
    101 State St.
    (413) 781–2420
  West Roxbury (H) 02132
    1400 VFW Parkway
    (617) 323–7700
  Worcester (OCS) 01601
    595 Main St.
    (617) 791–2251

Michigan
Allen Park (H&NHC) 48101
   Southfield & Outer Drive
   (313) 562–6000
Ann Arbor (H) 48105
   2215 Fuller Rd.
   (313) 769–7100
Battle Creek (H&NHC) 49016
   (616) 965–3281
Detroit (RO) 48226
   Patrick V. McNamara Federal Bldg.
   477 Michigan Ave.
If you live in the local telephone area of:
   Ann Arbor—662–2506
   Battle Creek—962–7568
   Bay City—894–4556
   Detroit—964–5110
   Flint—234–8646
   Grand Rapids—456–8511
   Jackson—787–7030
   Kalamazoo—344–0156
   Lansing/E. Lansing—484–7713
   Muskegon—726–4895
   Saginaw—754–7475
All other Michigan areas—
   (800) 482–0740
Grand Rapids (OCS) 49503
   260 Jefferson St., S.E.
   (616) 459–2200
Iron Mountain (H&NHC) 49801
   (906) 774–3300
Saginaw (H) 48602
   1500 Weiss St.
   (517) 793–2340

Minnesota
Minneapolis (H) 55417
   54th St. & 48th Ave., South
   (612) 725–6767
St. Cloud (H&NHC) 56301
   (612) 252–1670
St. Paul (C) 55111
   Federal Bldg., Fort Snelling

Minnesota *(continued)*

If you live in the local telephone area of:
Duluth—722–4467
Minneapolis—726–1454
Rochester—288–5888
St. Cloud—253–9300
St. Paul—726–1454
All other Minnesota areas—
(800) 692–2121
St. Paul (OCH) 55111
Fort Snelling
(612) 725–4131

Mississippi

Biloxi (H,D&NHC) 39531
(601) 388–5541
Jackson (H&NHC) 39216
1500 E. Woodrow Wilson Ave.
(601) 362–4471
Jackson (RO) 39204
Southport Office Building
2350 Highway 80 West
If you live in the local telephone area of:
Biloxi/Gulfport—432–5996
Jackson—969–4873
Meridian—693–6166
All other Mississippi areas—
(800) 682–5270

Missouri

Columbia (H&NHC) 65201
800 Stadium Road
(314) 443–2511
Kansas City (H) 64128
4801 Linwood Blvd.
(816) 861–4700
Kansas City (O) 64106
Federal Office Bldg.
601 E. 12th St.
(816) 758–3369
Poplar Bluff (H&NHC) 63901
(314) 686–4451
St. Louis (RO) 63103

Missouri *(continued)*
   Rm. 4600, Federal Bldg.
   1520 Market St.
   If you live in the local telephone area of:
   Columbia—449–1276
   Kansas City—861–3761
   St. Joseph—364–1171
   St. Louis—342–1171
   Springfield—883–7470
   All other Missouri areas—
   (800) 392–3761
   St. Louis (H&NHC) 63125
   915 N. Grand Blvd.
   (314) 487–0400

Montana
   Fort Harrison (RO) 59636
   If you live in the local telephone area of:
   Fort Harrison/Helena—442–6410
   Great Falls—761–3215
   All other Montana areas—
   (800) 332–6125
   Fort Harrison (H) 59636
   (406) 442–6410
   Miles City (H) 59301
   210 S. Winchester
   (406) 232–3060

Nebraska
   Grand Island (H) 68801
   2201 N. Broadway
   (308) 382–3660
   Lincoln (RO) 68508
   Federal Bldg.
   100 Centennial Mall North
   If you live in the local telephone area of:
   Lincoln—471–5001
   Omaha/Council Bluffs—221–3291
   All other Nebraska areas—
   (800) 742–7554
   Lincoln (H) 68510
   600 S. 70th St.
   (402) 867–6011
   Omaha (H) 68105

Nebraska *(continued)*
    4101 Woolworth Ave.
    (402) 346–8800

Nevada
    Henderson (OCS) 89015
        102 Lake Mead Dr.
        (702) 564–2420
    Reno (H) 89502
        1000 Locust St.
        (702) 329–1051
    Reno (RO) 89502
        1201 Terminal Way
    If you live in the local telephone area of:
        Las Vegas—386–2921
        Reno—329–9244
    All other Nevada areas—
        (800) 992–5740

New Hampshire
    Manchester (RO) 03103
        Norris Cotton Federal Bldg.
        275 Chestnut St.
    If you live in the local telephone area of:
        Manchester—666–7785
    All other New Hampshire areas—
        (800) 562–5260
    Manchester (H) 03104
        718 Smyth Rd.
        (603) 624–4366

New Jersey
    East Orange (H) 07019
        Tremont Ave. & S. Center
        (201) 676–1000
    Lyons (H) 07939
        (201) 647–0180
    Newark (RO) 07102
        20 Washington Place
    If you live in the local telephone area of:
        Atlantic City—348–8550
        Camden—541–8650
        Clifton/Patterson/Passaic—472–9632
        Long Branch/Asbury Park—870–2550

New Jersey *(continued)*
 New Brunswick/Sayreville—828–5600
 Newark—645–2150
 Perth Amboy—442–5300
 Trenton—989–8116
All other New Jersey areas—
 (800) 242–5867
Newark (OCH) 07102
 20 Washington Place
 (201) 645–3491

New Mexico
 Albuquerque (RO) 87102
  Dennis Chavez Federal Bldg.
  U.S. Courthouse
  500 Gold Ave., S.W.
 If you live in the local telephone area of:
  Albuquerque—766–3361
 All other New Mexico areas—
  (800) 432–6853
 Albuquerque (H&NHC) 87108
  2100 Ridgecrest Dr., S.E.
  (505) 265–1711

New York
 Albany (H&NHC) 12208
  113 Holland Ave.
  (518) 462–3311
 Albany (O) 12207
  Leo W. O'Brien Federal Bldg.
  Clinton Ave. & N. Pearl St.
  (518) 562–4206
 Batavia (H) 14020
  Redfield Pkwy.
  (716) 343–7500
 Bath (H,D&NHC) 14810
  (607) 776–2111
 Bronx (H) 10468
  130 W. Kingsbridge Rd.
  (212) 584–9000
 Brooklyn (H&NHC) 11209
  800 Poly Place
  (212) 836–6600
 Brooklyn (OC) 11205

New York *(continued)*
    35 Ryerson St.
    (212) 330–7500
  Buffalo (RO) 14202
    Federal Bldg.
    111 W. Huron
  If you live in the local telephone area of:
    Binghamton—772–0856
    Buffalo—846–5191
    Elmira—734–4171
    Rome—339–0400
    Utica—735–6431
  All other areas of Western New York State—
    (800) 462–1130
  Buffalo (H&NHC) 14215
    3495 Bailey Ave.
    (716) 834–9200
  Canandaigua (H&NHC) 14424
    Ft. Hill Ave.
    (716) 394–2000
  Castle Point (H&NHC) 12511
    (914) 831–2000
  Montrose (H&NHC) 10548
    (914) 737–4400
  New York City (H) 10010
    1st Ave. at E. 24th St.
    (212) 686–7500
  New York City (RO) 10001
    252 Seventh Ave.
  Counties of Albany, Bronx,
    Clinton, Columbia, Delaware,
    Dutchess, Essex, Franklin,
    Fulton, Greene, Hamilton,
    Kings, Montgomery, Nassau,
    New York, Orange, Otsego,
    Putnam, Queens, Rensselaer,
    Richmond, Rockland,
    Saratoga, Schenectady,
    Schoharie, Suffolk, Sullivan,
    Ulster, Warren, Washington,
    Westchester.
  If you live in the local telephone area of:
    Hempstead—483–6188
    New York—620–6901
    Poughkeepsie—452–5330

New York *(continued)*
Scarsdale—723–7476
All other areas in the above counties—
(800) 442–5882
New York City (OCH) 10001
252 7th Ave. at 24th St.
(212) 620–6776
New York City (Prosthetic Center) 10001
252 7th Ave.
(212) 620–6636
Northport (H) 11768
Long Island - Middleville Rd.
(516) 261-4400
Rochester (O&OCS) 14614
Federal Office Bldg. and
Courthouse
100 State St.
(716) 263–5740 (O)
(716) 263–5734 (OCS)
Syracuse (O) 13202
U.S. Courthouse and
Federal Building
100 S. Clinton St.
(315) 950–5532
Syracuse (Mental Hygiene Clinic) 13202
Gateway Bldg.
803 S. Salina St.
(315) 473–2619
Syracuse (H&NHC) 13210
Irving Ave. & University Pl.
(315) 476–7461

North Carolina
Asheville (H&NHC) 28805
(704) 298–7911
Durham (H) 27705
508 Fulton St.
(919) 286–0411
Fayetteville (H&NHC) 28301
2300 Ramsey St.
(919) 488–2120
Salisbury (H&NHC) 28144
1601 Brenner Ave.
(704) 636–2351

North Carolina *(continued)*
    Winston-Salem (OCH) 27102
        Federal Bldg.
        251 N. Main St.
        (919) 761–3562
    Winston-Salem (RO) 27102
        Federal Bldg.
        251 N. Main St.
    If you live in the local telephone area of:
        Asheville—253–6861
        Charlotte—375–9351
        Durham—683–1367
        Fayetteville—323–1242
        Greensboro—274–1994
        High Point—887–1202
        Raleigh—821–1166
        Winston-Salem—748–1800
    All other North Carolina areas—
        (800) 642–0841

North Dakota
    Fargo (RO) 58102
        21st Ave. & Elm St.
    If you live in the local telephone area of:
        Fargo—293–3080
        All other North Dakota areas
        (800) 342–4790
    Fargo (H&NHC) 58102
        2101 Elm St.
        (701) 232–3241

Ohio
    Brecksville (H&NHC) 44141
        10000 Brecksville Rd.
        (216) 526–3030
    Chillicothe (H&NHC) 45601
        (614) 773–1141
    Cincinnati (H&NHC) 45220
        3200 Vine St.
        (513) 773–0225
    Cincinnati (O) 45202
        Rm. 1024, Federal Off. Bldg.
        550 Main St.
        (513) 684–2600

Ohio *(continued)*
Cleveland (H) 44106
    10701 E. Boulevard
    (216) 791–3800
Cleveland (RO) 44199
    Anthony J. Celebrezze
    Federal Office Bldg.
    1240 E. 9th St.
If you live in the local telephone area of:
    Akron—535–3327
    Canton—453–8113
    Cincinnati—579–0505
    Cleveland—621–5050
    Columbus—224–8872
    Dayton—223–1394
    Springfield—322–4907
    Toledo—241–6223
    Warren—399–8985
    Youngstown—744–4383
    All other Ohio areas—
    (800) 362–9024
Columbus (O) 43215
    Rm. 309 Fed. Bldg.
    200 N. High St.
    (614) 469–7334
Columbus (OC) 43210
    456 Clinic Drive
    (614) 469–5664
Dayton (H,D&NHC) 45428
    4100 W. 3rd St.
    (513) 268–6511

Oklahoma
Muskogee (H) 74401
    Memorial Station
    Honor Heights Dr.
    (918) 683–3261
Muskogee (RO) 74401
    Federal Bldg.
    125 S. Main St.
If you live in the local telephone area of:
    Lawton—357–2400
    Muskogee—687–2500
    Oklahoma City—235–2641

Oklahoma *(continued)*
>Stillwater—377–1770
>Tulsa—583–5891
>All other Oklahoma areas—
>(800) 482–2800
>Oklahoma City (O) 73102
>>200 N.W. 4th St.
>>(405) 231–4115
>Oklahoma City (H) 73104
>>921 N.E. 13th St.
>>(405) 272–9876

Oregon
>Portland (H) 97207
>>Sam Jackson Park
>>(503) 222–9221
>Portland (RO) 97204
>>Federal Bldg.
>>1220 SW. 3rd Avenue
>If you live in the local telephone area of:
>>Eugene/Springfield—342–8274
>>Portland—221–2431
>>Salem—581–9343
>All other Oregon areas—
>(800) 452–7276
>Portland (OCH) 97204
>>426 S.W. Stark St.
>>(503) 221–2575
>>Roseburg (H&NHC) 97470
>>(503) 672–4411
>White City (D) 97501
>>(503) 826–2111

Pennsylvania
>Altoona (H&NHC) 16603
>>Pleasant Valley Blvd.
>>(814) 943–8164
>Butler (H&NHC) 16001
>>(412) 287–4781
>Coatesville (H&NHC) 19320
>>Black Horse Rd.
>>(215) 384–7711
>Erie (H&NHC) 16501

Pennsylvania *(continued)*
    135 E. 38th St. Blvd.
    (814) 868–8661
Harrisburg (OCS) 17108
    Federal Bldg.
    228 Walnut St.
    (717) 782–4590
Lebanon (H&NHC) 17042
    (717) 272–6621
Philadelphia (H) 19104
    University & Woodland Aves.
    (215) 382–2201
Philadelphia (OCH) 19102
    1421 Cherry St.
    (215) 597–3311
    Ask for OCH
Philadelphia (C) 19101
    P.O. Box 8079
    5000 Wissahickon Ave.
Counties of Adams, Berks,
    Bradford, Bucks, Cameron,
    Carbon, Centre, Chester,
    Clinton, Columbia, Cumberland,
    Dauphin, Delaware, Franklin,
    Juniata, Lackawanna,
    Lancaster, Lebanon, Lehigh,
    Luzerne, Lycoming, Mifflin,
    Monroe, Montgomery,
    Montour, Northampton,
    Northumberland, Perry,
    Philadelphia, Pike, Potter,
    Schuylkill, Snyder, Sullivan,
    Susquehanna, Tioga, Union,
    Wayne, Wyoming, and York:
If you live in the local telephone area of:
    Allentown/Bethlehem/Easton—821–6823
    Harrisburg—232–6677
    Lancaster—394–0596
    Philadelphia—438–5225
    Reading—376–6548
    Scranton—961–3883
    Wilkes-Barre—824–4636
    Williamsport—322–4649
    York—845–6686
All other areas in the above counties—(800) 822–3920

Pennsylvania *(continued)*
Pittsburgh (RO) 15222
1000 Liberty Ave.
If you live in the local telephone area of:
Altoona—944–7101
Johnstown—535–8625
Pittsburgh—281–4233
All other areas in Western
Pennsylvania—(800) 242–0233
Pittsburgh (OCH) 15222
1000 Liberty Ave.
(412) 644–6750
Pittsburgh (H&NHC) 15240
University Drive C.
(412) 683–3000
Pittsburgh (H) 15206
Highland Drive
(412) 363–4900
Wilkes-Barre (O) 18701
19–27 N. Main St.
(717) 592–6226
Wilkes-Barre (H) 18711
1111 E. End Blvd.
(717) 824–3521

Philippines
Manila (RO) 96528
1131 Roxas Blvd. (Manila)
AOP San Francisco (Air Mail)

Puerto Rico
Ponce (OCS) 00731
Calle Isabel No. 60
(809) 843–5151
San Juan (H) 00921
Barrio Monacillos
Rio Piedras GPO Box 4867
(809) 763–0418
San Juan (RO) 00918
U.S. Courthouse & Fed. Bldg.
Carlos E. Chardon St.
Hato Rey
(809) 763–4141

Rhode Island
Providence (RO) 02903
321 S. Main St.
If you live in the local telephone area of:
Providence—528–4431
All other Rhode Island areas—
Ask operator for Enterprise 5050
Providence (H) 02908
Davis Park
(401) 521–1700

South Carolina
Charleston (H) 29407
109 Bee St.
(803) 722–5011
Columbia (RO) 29201
1801 Assembly St.
If you live in the local telephone area of:
Charleston—723–5581
Columbia—765–5861
Greenville—232–2457
All other South Carolina areas—(800) 922–1000
Columbia (H&NHC) 29201
Garners Ferry Rd.
(803) 776–4000
Greenville (OCS) 29607
Piedmont East Bldg.
37 Villa Road
(803) 232–7303

South Dakota
Fort Meade (H) 57741
(605) 347–2511
Hot Springs (H&D) 57747
(605) 745–4101
Sioux Falls (H&NHC) 57101
2501 W. 22nd St.
(605) 782–3201
Sioux Falls (RO) 57101
Courthouse Plaza Bldg.
300 North Dakota Ave.
If you live in the local telephone area of:
Sioux Falls—336–3496

South Dakota *(continued)*
All other South Dakota areas—
(800) 952–3550

Tennessee
Chattanooga (OCS) 37411
Bldg. 6300 East Gate Center
(615) 266–3151
Knoxville (OCS) 37920
Baptist Prof. Bldg.
200 Blount Ave.
(615) 637–9300
Memphis (H) 38104
1030 Jefferson Ave.
(901) 523–8990
Mountain Home (H,D&NHC) 37684
Johnson City
(615) 928–0281
Murfreesboro (H&NHC) 37130
(615) 893–1360
Nashville (RO) 37203
110 9th Ave., S.
If you live in the local telephone area of:
Chattanooga—267–6587
Knoxville—546–5700
Memphis—527–4583
Nashville—254–5411
All other Tennessee areas—
(800) 342–8330
Nashville (H) 37203
1310 24th Ave., S.
(615) 327–4751

Texas
Amarillo (H) 79106
6010 Amarillo Blvd., W.
(806) 355–9703
Big Spring (H&NHC) 79720
2400 S. Gregg St.
(915) 263–7361
Bonham (H,D&NHC) 75418
Ninth & Lipscomb
(214) 583–2111
Corpus Christi (OCS) 78404

Texas *(continued)*
>1502 S. Brownlee Blvd.
>(512) 888–3251

>Dallas (O) 75202
>>U.S. Courthouse and
>>Fed. Office Bldg.
>>1100 Commerce St.
>>(214) 749–3207

>Dallas (H) 75216
>>4500 S. Lancaster Rd.
>>(214) 376–5451

>El Paso (OC) 79925
>>5919 Brook Hollow Dr.
>>(915) 543–7890

>Houston (RO) 77054
>>2515 Murworth Dr.

>Counties of Angelina, Aransas, Atascosa, Austin, Bandera, Bee, Bexar, Blanco, Brazoria, Brewster, Brooks, Caldwell, Calhoun, Cameron, Chambers, Colorado, Comal, Crockett, DeWitt, Dimmitt, Duval, Edwards, Fort Bend, Frio, Galveston, Gillespie, Goliad, Gonzales, Grimes, Guadalupe, Hardin, Harris, Hays, Hidalgo, Houston, Jackson, Jasper, Jefferson, Jim Hogg, Jim Wells, Karnes, Kendall, Kenedy, Kerr, Kimble, Kinney, Kleberg, LaSalle, Lavaca, Liberty, Live Oak, McCulloch, McMullen, Mason, Matagorda, Maverick, Medina, Menard, Montgomery, Nacogdoches, Newton, Nueces, Orange, Pecos, Polk, Real, Refugio, Sabine, San Augustine, San Jacinto, San Patricio, Schleicher, Shelby, Starr, Sutton, Terrell, Trinity, Tyler, Uvalde, Val Verde, Victoria, Walker, Waller, Washington, Webb, Wharton,

Texas *(continued)*

Willacy, Wilson, Zapata,
Zavala:
If you live in the local telephone area of:
Beaumont—838–6222
Corpus Christi—884–1994
Edinburg/McAllen/Pharr—383–8168
Houston—664–4664
San Antonio—226–7661
Texas City/Galveston—948–3011
All other areas in the above counties—
(800) 392–2200
Houston (H&NHC) 77211
2002 Holcombe Blvd.
(713) 747–3000
Kerrville (H&NHC) 78028
(512) 896–2020
Lubbock (O&OC) 79401
Federal Building
1205 Texas Ave., Room 814
(806) 762–7415
Marlin (H) 76661
1016 Ward St.
(817) 883–3511
McAllen (OCS) 78501
1220 Jackson Ave.
(512) 682–2443
San Antonio (H) 78284
7440 Merton Minter Blvd.
(512) 696–9660
San Antonio (O) 78285
410 S. Main St.
(512) 730–6925
San Antonio (OC) 78285
307 Dwyer Ave.
(512) 225–5511
Temple (H&D) 76501
1901 S. First
(817) 778–4811
Waco (RO) 76710
1400 N. Valley Mills Dr.
If you live in the local telephone area of:
Abilene—673–5286
Amarillo—376–7202
Austin—477–5831

Texas *(continued)*
    Dallas—824–5440
    El Paso—545–2500
    Ft. Worth—336–1641
    Killeen—699–2351
    Lubbock—747–5256
    Midland/Odessa/Terminal—563–0324
    Waco—772–3060
    Wichita Falls—723–7103
All other areas in Texas—(800) 792–1110
Waco (H&NHC) 76703
    Memorial Drive
    (817) 752–6581
Waco (OCH) 76710
    1400 N. Valley Mills Dr.
    (817) 756–6511

Utah
    Salt Lake City (RO) 84138
    Federal Bldg.
    125 S. State St.
If you live in the local telephone area of:
    Ogden—399–4433
    Provo/Orem—375–2902
    Salt Lake City—524–5960
All other Utah areas—(800) 662–9163
Salt Lake City (H&NHC) 84113
    500 Foothill Drive
    (801) 582–1565

Vermont
    White River Junction (RO) 05001
If you live in the local telephone area of:
    White River Junction—295–9363
All other Vermont areas—
    (800) 622–4134
White River Junction (H,NHC) 05001
    (802) 295–9363

Virginia
    Hampton (H,D&NHC) 23667
    (804) 723–6501
    Richmond (H) 23249

Virginia *(continued)*
1201 Broad Rock Rd.
(804) 231–9011
Northern Virginia
Counties of Arlington and Fairfax and the cities of Alexandria, Fairfax, and
Falls Church:
Washington, DC (RO) 20421
941 N. Capitol St., N.E.
If you live in the above Virginia counties or cities—
872–1151
Roanoke (RO) 24011
210 Franklin Rd., SW.
If you live in the local telephone area of:
Hampton—722–7477
Norfolk—627–0441
Richmond—648–1621
Roanoke—982–6440
All other Virginia areas—(800) 542–5826
Salem (H&NHC) 24153
(703) 982–2463

Washington
Seattle (RO) 98174
Federal Office Bldg.
915 2nd Ave.
If you live in the local telephone area of:
Everett—259–9232
Seattle—624–7200
Spokane—747–3041
Tacoma—383–3851
Yakima—248–7970
All other Washington areas—
(800) 552–7480
Seattle (H) 98108
4435 Beacon Ave., S.
(206) 762–1010
Seattle (OCH) 98104
Smith Tower, 2nd & Yesler
(206) 442–5030
Spokane (H) 99208
N. 4815 Assembly St.
(509) 328–4521
Tacoma (H&NCH) 98493
American Lake

Washington *(continued)*
    (206) 588–2185
    Vancouver (H) 98661
    (206) 696–4061
    Walla Walla (H) 99362
    77 Wainwright Dr.
    (509) 525–5200

West Virginia
    Beckley (H&NHC) 25801
    200 Veterans Ave.
    (304) 253–8383
    Clarksburg (H) 26301
    (304) 923–3411
    Counties of Brooke, Hancock,
    Marshall and Ohio:
    Pittsburgh, PA (RO) 15222
    1000 Liberty Ave.
    If you live in the local telephone area of:
    Wheeling—232–1431
    Other: (800) 642–3520
    (Huntington, WV RO)
    Remaining counties in West Virginia served by:
    Huntington (RO) 25701
    502 Eighth St.
    If you live in the local telephone area of:
    Charleston—344–3531
    Huntington—522–8294
    All other areas in West Virginia—
    (800) 642–3520
    Huntington (H) 25701
    1540 Spring Valley Dr.
    (304) 429–1381
    Martinsburg (H&D) 25401
    (304) 263–0266
    Wheeling (OCS) 26003
    11th & Chapline Sts.
    (304) 234–0123

Wisconsin
    Madison (H) 53705
    2500 Overlook Terrace
    (608) 256–1901
    Milwaukee (RO) 53202

Wisconsin *(continued)*
    342 N. Water St.
    If you live in the local telephone area of:
    Green Bay—437–9001
    Madison—257–5467
    Milwaukee—278–8680
    Racine—637–6743
    All other Wisconsin areas—
    (800) 242–9025
    Tomah (H&NHC) 54660
    (608) 372–3971
    Wood (H,D&NHC) 53193
    500 W. National Ave.
    (414) 384–2000

Wyoming
    Cheyenne (RO) 82001
    2360 E. Pershing Blvd.
    If you live in the local telephone area of:
    Cheyenne—778–7550
    All other Wyoming areas—
    (800) 442–2761
    Cheyenne (H&NHC) 82001
    2360 E. Pershing Blvd.
    (307) 778–7550
    Sheridan (H) 82801
    (307) 672–3473

New Federal Regulations Are Intended to Curb Abuses by Vocational Schools

Many vocational schools direct their advertising to veterans and thereby manage to obtain not only VA benefits but federally guaranteed loans.

Michael Pertschuk, chairman of the Federal Trade Commission, warns that many student defaults are attributable to fraud and deception by vocational schools. "Students who are lured into vocational courses with false promises of better jobs and higher salaries often drop out and then default on their loans."

Consequently, the government has issued regulations intended to protect all students against fraud and deception by private vocational schools.

Even though the new regulations do not take effect until January 1, 1980, you should keep them in mind when you look for a good vocational school. Ask the schools you visit how many of their students drop out of school, how many graduates they actually place and what salaries they earn.

If a school is not interested in giving out this information, perhaps you should consider looking for another school.

The new regulations apply to schools that offer courses such as stenography, computer programming, car mechanics and cosmetology.

The regulations provide that:

1. A school must give refunds to students who drop courses for instruction that they did not receive. (The school will be allowed to keep $75 to cover administrative costs.)

2. A school must allow a student a fourteen-day cooling-off period after a contract is signed, during which time the student can get a full refund from the school.

3. A school must disclose specific job placement rates and earnings if advertisements for the school promise high salaries and good jobs or make similar claims.

Counseling by the VA Is Available to Veterans

The VA offers counseling in many areas and may be of help in answering your questions about the vocational school you are interested in.

The VA also offers educational and vocational counseling, tutorial assistance, reader service and other special help in training that you may need.

The VA provides a special vocational rehabilitation program to help disabled veterans select, prepare for and secure work in line with their personal goals, interests, abilities and physical capabilities.

When you have completed your training, the VA can help you in job placement and job adjustment.

Vietnam veterans should remember that they have a deadline for applying for benefits. Your eligibility ends ten years after discharge or no later than December 31, 1989.

Veterans who find a school or college that interests them should check the school's credibility with their guidance counselor or consult one of the many excellent books published on this subject.

One such book is the *Comparative Guide to American Colleges* by James Cass and Max Birnbaum, published by Harper & Row and now in its eighth edition. This is a consumer-oriented guide to colleges that gives such important information as the percentage of graduates who go on to graduate school, the number of students who drop out of school after their freshman year, the number of professors who hold doctorates, the size of the library—all considerations that are important in choosing a college.

18

Don't Work Your Way Through College
If You're Related to a Veteran

I worked my way through college—eight years of back-breaking, starving reality. Many people will say that does a lot for your character, and I suppose it does.

But if I had only realized that I didn't have to work so hard! For all the time there was a scholarship for children of veterans of World War I, and my father had been in World War I and had even won a Purple Heart and a Silver Star.

How could I not have known?

No one told me, and I didn't know enough to ask. I was president of the American Legion Junior Auxiliary, Syracuse Downtown Post, I went to Girls State and still I didn't know enough to ask.

If you are related to a veteran of World War I—your grandfather, perhaps—here's a scholarship that you should take note of.

The La Verne Noyles Scholarship

The purpose of the La Verne Noyles Scholarship is to express gratitude to, and to some degree to reward, those who offered the supreme sacrifice of life for the United States in World War I.

These scholarships provide for the payment of tuition, in part or in full, of deserving students who need assistance to obtain university or college training.

The scholarships are awarded without regard to sex, race, religion or political party only to those citizens of the United States who are descended by blood from someone who served

199

in the United States Army or Navy in World War I and whose service was terminated by death or honorable discharge.

Eligible students may make application for the award directly to the following universities and colleges.

Amherst College, Amherst, MA 01002
Beloit College, Beloit, WI 53511
Bradley University, Peoria, IL 61625
California Institute of Technology, Pasadena, CA 91125
Coe College, Cedar Rapids, IA 52404
Cornell College, Mount Vernon, IA 52314
Cornell University, Ithaca, NY 14850
Denison University, Granville, OH 43023
George Peabody College for Teachers, Nashville, TN 37203
Grinnell College, Grinnell, IA 50112
Howard University, Washington, DC 20001
Illinois College, Jacksonville, IL 62650
Illinois Institute of Technology, Chicago, IL 60616
Illinois Wesleyan University, Bloomington, IL 61701
Indiana University at Bloomington, IN 47401
Iowa State University of Science and Technology, Ames, IA 50010
Kansas State University, Manhattan, KS 66506
Knox College, Galesburg, IL 61401
Lawrence University, Appleton, WI 54911
Michigan State University, East Lansing, MI 48823
Monmouth College, Monmouth, IL 61462
New Mexico State University, University Park, NM 88001
North Dakota State University, Fargo, ND 58102
Northwestern University, Evanston, IL 60201
Oberlin College, Oberlin, OH 44704
Oklahoma State University of Agriculture and Applied Science, Stillwater, OK 74074
Purdue University, West Lafayette, IN 47907
South Dakota State University, Brookings, SD 57006
Southern Methodist University, Dallas, TX 75275
Texas Technical University, Lubbock, TX 79409
University of Alabama, University, AL 35486

University of California, Berkeley, CA 94720
University of Chicago, Chicago, IL 60637
University of Colorado, Boulder, CO 80302
University of Illinois, Urbana, IL 61801
University of Iowa, Iowa City, IA 52240
University of Kansas, Lawrence, KS 66044
University of Michigan, Ann Arbor, MI 48104
University of Minnesota, Minneapolis, MN 55455
University of Missouri, Columbia, MO 65201
University of Nebraska, Lincoln, NE 68508
University of North Dakota, Grand Forks, ND 58202
University of Oklahoma, Norman, OK 73069
University of Southern California, Los Angeles, CA 90007
University of Texas, Austin, TX 78712
University of Wisconsin, Madison, WI 53706
Wabash College, Crawfordsville, IN 47933
Washington University, St. Louis, MO 63130

First Marine Division Association Scholarship

The First Marine Division Association, Inc., offers surviving dependents a scholarship to further their education. Grants are based on financial need and are awarded for a four-year college course (or less, as the case may be). Grants are not given for graduate study.

Applicants must be dependents of persons, now deceased from any cause or totally disabled due to wounds received in action, who served in the First Marine Division or in a unit attached to the First Marine Division.

When applying, applicants should include full name, service number and social security number of their deceased or disabled relative. For information, write the First Marine Division Association, Inc., 1704 Florida Avenue, Woodbridge, VA 22191.

Second Marine Division Association Scholarship

A Memorial Scholarship Fund is administered by the Second Marine Division Association that provides scholarship grants of up to $400 per year for four years.

The applicant must be a surviving dependent child of a person who served in the Second Marine Division or in a unit attached to the Second Marine Division and who, while serving, lost his or her life in the service of the United States or as a direct result of such service.

For information, write the Second Marine Division Association, P. O. Box 113, Willow Springs, IL 60408.

Third Marine Division Association Scholarship

Three memorial scholarships—the Third Marine Division Association Scholarship Fund, the Major General Bruno A. Hochmuth, USMC, Scholarship and the General Graves B. Erskine, USMC, Scholarship—are administered by the Third Marine Division Association.

Grants are awarded in amounts of $400 to $1,200 per scholastic year for up to four years, based on need and performance.

Applicant must be a dependent of a military person and be between the ages of seventeen and twenty-six at the time of the initial award. Applicants must apply by April 15 of the year of their matriculation.

For information, write the Secretary, Scholarship Fund, Third Marine Division Association, 7222 Valley Crest Boulevard, Annandale, VA 22003.

Fourth Marine Division Association Scholarship

The Fourth Marine Division provides scholarships and education benefits for the children of persons who served in the Fourth Marine Division or in an attached unit.

Funds are granted in the amount of $1,000 annually, for a period not to exceed four years.

Children of persons who served with the Fourth Marine Division or an attached unit and who, while serving or subsequently, became deceased or disabled are eligible for the scholarship.

For information, write Lt. Col. G. D. Pines, USMC, Rtd., Chairman, Scholarship Committee, 1508 Laurel Road, Oceanside, CA 92054

Applications must be received no later than June 1.

Fifth Marine Division Scholarship Association

The Fifth Marine Division Association provides scholarships of up to $1,000 per year for a total of four years.

Applicants must be high school graduates or the equivalent and enrolled in, or eligible for entry in, an accredited liberal arts or technical or vocational institution. An applicant must be the son or daughter of someone who served with the Fifth Marine Division.

Applications must be submitted no later than May 15 prior to the academic year of study. For information, write John Jaqua, Chairman, Scholarship Fund, P.O. Box 1089, Portland, OR 47371.

Society of the First Division Scholarship

This scholarship awards a son or daughter of a First Division veteran or a member of the First Infantry Division who, upon honorable discharge from service, intends to further his education.

Awards of $1,000 are payable in four annual installments of $250 each. The number of awards each year will be determined by the amount of money available to the fund.

For information, write the Society of the First Division, 5 Montgomery Avenue, Erdenheim, Philadelphia, PA 19118.

Disabled American Veterans Scholarship

The Disabled American Veterans offer a four-year scholarship to the children of veterans with a service-connected disability whose parents are deceased or otherwise unable to provide them with a college education.

Scholarships may be granted to those presently attending college, provided they meet the specific criteria for participation in the program.

The scholarship may be used at any accredited college. High verbal and math scores on the SAT are required of all applicants. Rank in class and a parent's confidential questionnaire are used to establish financial need.

For information, write Denvel D. Adams, assistant national adjutant, Disabled American Veterans National Headquarters, P.O. Box 14301, Cincinnati, OH 45214.

19

Scholarships for Children
of Veterans and Nonveterans

"No student should decide he cannot afford to continue his education beyond high school."

These are the words of Mike Ayers, the Editor of *Need a Lift?*, the American Legion scholarship handbook.

Because the American Legion considers its handbook a service to the young people of the nation, the handbook lists college scholarships available to all students, the children of veterans and nonveterans alike.

In this chapter we describe some of the scholarships and fellowships listed in the Legion handbook.

SCHOLARSHIP AWARDS

H. J. Heinz Company Scholarship Program

Applicants for the B.A. degree must be completing the first year of a four-year program or completing the first or second year at a junior or community college and planning to continue in a B.A. program.

The maximum value of each senior college award is $3,300. Junior or community college scholarship awards of up to $1,700 are given to students in programs leading to an associate degree in foodservice management. Applicants for the community college award must be high school seniors who will be attending a community college during the scholarship year.

For information, write the National Institute for the Foodservice Industry, 120 South Riverside Plaza, Chicago, IL 60606.

The application deadline each year is April 1.

Golden Plate Scholarship Program

The award is sponsored by the International Foodservice Manufacturers Association Education Foundation. Applicants must be students enrolled or ing to enroll in a foodservice program in a junior or community college, senior college or graduate school. Each scholarship is $600 for one academic year.

For information, write the National Institute for the Foodservice Industry, 120 South Riverside Plaza, Chicago, IL 60606.

Bell & Howell Schools Scholarship Program

The award, sponsored by Bell & Howell Schools, is for high school graduates from the United States who wish to attend one of the Bell & Howell schools.

Fifty-five full tuition scholarships in electronics engineering technology are awarded; selection is made on the basis of an essay and applicant's high school academic record.

For information, write Bell & Howell, Administrative Offices, 2201 West Howard Street, Evanston, IL 60202.

The Material Handling Institute Educational Foundation, Inc.

Scholarships are awarded to students in accredited programs that include an emphasis on material handling, through direct and related courses and through independent study.

The scholarships vary in number and value. Students must have completed at least two years of a B.A. program or be commencing graduate study; they must be United States citizens and have at least a B average.

For information, write the Material Handling Institute Educational Foundation, Inc., 1326 Freeport Road, Pittsburgh, PA 15238.

The application deadline is February 1.

National 4-H Council Scholarships

A total of 270 scholarships, from $500 to $1,000 in value, are available to present and former 4-H members who are enrolled in college. Applicants must have an interest in one of the following fields: animal science; agronomy, soils, entomology, plant pathology or horticulture; veterinary medicine; or agricultural business, economics and marketing.

For information, write the 4-H Leader at a state land-grant university, or information may be obtained from the National 4-H Council, 150 North Wacker Drive, Chicago, IL 60606.

The National Coal Association

The coal industry offers scholarships to high school seniors. Information concerning the value of the scholarships can be obtained by writing the Education Division, National Coal Association, 1130 17th Street, N.W., Washington, D.C. 20036.

The National Easter Seal Society for Crippled Children and Adults

Scholarships are available for specialized training to work with the physically handicapped. Information regarding the scholarships may be obtained by writing the National Easter Seal Society, 2–23 Ogden Avenue, Chicago, IL 60612.

The National Association of Secondary School Principals and the National Honor Society.

Awards have a value of $1,000 each; a total of $225,000 in scholarship money is available to high school seniors who are members of the National Honor Society.

For information, write the National Association of Secondary School Principals, 1904 Association Drive, Reston, VA 22091

Science Talent Search

Sponsored by Westinghouse Electric and the Westinghouse Educational Foundation, the Science Talent Institute offers scholarships to young men and women in their senior year of high school.

Ten scholarships are awarded, their value ranging from $4,000 to $10,000, on the basis of high school record, national test scores, a thousand-word report on an independent science research project and interviews with the judges at the Science Talent Institute in Washington, D.C. Personal data sheet must be completed by teachers, principal and student. A report on the student's research project must be submitted.

In addition to the ten scholarship awards, thirty other finalists receive $250 each. For information, write Science Clubs of America, Science Service, Inc., 1719 N Street, N.W., Washington, D.C. 20036.

Amoco Foundation, Inc., Scholarships

Amoco offers scholarships to students who plan to study petroleum engineering, geophysics, geology or engineering. Awards start at $700 for freshmen and increase $100 each year, providing a total of $3,400 for four years.

For information, write the Amoco Foundation, Inc., 200 East Randolph Drive, Chicago, IL 60601.

The Elks Foundation Scholarship Awards

For the 1978–1979 school year, the total value of the Elks awards was $808,880. This amount provided 1,100 students with scholarships ranging from $600 to $3,000.

Any student in senior high school who has an Order of Elks Club in his or her community may file an application. Application blanks should be obtained from an officer of the local Elks Lodge or the secretary of the state Elks Association. Applications must be filed before February 10 each year.

Rotary Foundation Scholarships

These are available to graduate or undergraduate students, journalists, teachers of the handicapped and students in technical training programs between the ages of eighteen and fifty. Awards are for one year's study in a country other than the recipient's own.

The scholarship provides school fees, room and board, transportation and expenses for limited travel during the year. Contact your local Rotary Club for details.

Applications must be received by March 1.

The Shell Companies Foundation, Inc.

Shell offers ten Shell Merit Scholarships and ten Shell Achievement Scholarships annually through the National Merit Scholarship Corporation, which administers the program. The scholarships are for high school seniors who plan careers as teachers of high school science or mathematics; Achievement Scholarships are for qualified black high school graduates who plan careers in the business or technical field.

For information, write the National Merit Scholarship Corporation, One American Plaza, Evanston, IL 60201.

Western Golf Association

Scholarships are awarded annually to qualified caddies who rank in the top one-fourth of their class. A total of 240 four-year scholarships are available to those who have caddied for a minimum of two years.

For information, write the Evans Scholars Foundation, Western Golf Association, Golf, IL 60029.

Westinghouse Educational Family Scholarships

Four $8,000 and forty $1,500 scholarships are awarded annually to children of Westinghouse employees, where the student's parent is or was (if deceased or retired) employed. For information, write University Relations Office, Westinghouse Electric Corp., Pittsburgh, PA 15221.

Bertha Lamme Scholarship

This award is sponsored by Westinghouse and is given to young women entering engineering as freshmen. For information, write the Society of Women Engineers, United Engineering Center, Room 305, 345 East 47th Street, New York, NY 10017.

National Achievement Scholarship Program for Outstanding Negro Students

Five $1,000 scholarships are awarded.

Applicants must reside in the United States, and applications must be submitted during the *fall* months of the senior year.

For information, write the National Merit Scholarship Corp., Evanston, IL 60201.

The Cooper Union for the Advancement of Science and Art Scholarships

There are 230 free tuition scholarships, each valued at from $2,000 to $2,500 per year. Applicants must compete for admission to the Cooper Union School of Art, School of Architecture or School of Engineering. The scholarships continue to graduation as long as the student maintains required academic standards. Scholarships are available to students with superior high school records.

For information, write the Dean of Admissions, The Cooper Union, Cooper Square, New York, NY 10003.

National Presbyterian College Scholarships

Offered in the fall of each year by the United Presbyterian Church, U.S.A., to qualified young Presbyterian people entering as freshmen any United Presbyterian church-related college. There are eighty scholarships, ranging in value from $100 to $1,400. Applicants do not have to show financial need.

For information, write National Presbyterian College Scholarships, Vocational Agency, United Presbyterian Church, U.S.A., 475 Riverside Drive, New York, NY 10027.

Knights of Columbus "Pro Deo and Pro Patria Scholarship"

The Knights of Columbus have established scholarships for sons and daughters of living or deceased members. The $1,000 awards may be renewed annually, subject to satisfactory academic performance.

For information, write the Director of Scholarship Aid, Knights of Columbus, Supreme Council, P.O. Drawer 16701, Columbus Plaza, New Haven, CT 06507.

Final filing date for applications is March 1.

American Fund for Dental Health Scholarships for Minority Students

The awards have a value of up to $4,500 over a two-year period. Students must be United States citizens, members of a minority group that is underrepresented in the dental profession and entering their first year of dental school.

Information and applications can be obtained at the Financial Aid office of the dental school you plan to attend. The deadline is April 15.

Dental Laboratory Technology Scholarships

The American Fund for Dental Health also sponsors these awards, whose value ranges from $500 to $650. The deadline is June 1.

For information, write the American Association of Dental Schools, 1625 Massachusetts Avenue, N.W., Washington, D.C. 20036.

The Colgate University Alumni Memorial Scholarships

Thirty scholarships are offered, with an annual value of $100 to $5,000, to freshmen entering Colgate University. The deadline for filing is February 1.

For information, write the Director of Admissions, Colgate University, Hamilton, NY 13346.

The Allstate Foundation Scholarships

These are nursing education scholarships for 300 students; they cover tuition expenses.

For information, write the National League for Nursing, 10 Columbus Circle, New York, NY 10019.

FELLOWSHIP AWARDS

Fellowships are gifts of money to graduate and professional students. The number of fellowships available is small, compared to the number and variety of scholarships offered.

The Daniel and Florence Guggenheim Foundation Fellowships

These fellowships are offered to scientists and engineers for graduate study in energy conversion, transportation, jet propulsion, space flight and flight structure. The ten fellowships have stipends ranging up to $4,000, depending on the level of advancement of the student, plus tuition.

The fellowships are to be used for study at the Daniel and Florence Guggenheim Jet Propulsion Center at the California Institute of Technology, the Daniel and Florence Guggenheim Institute of Flight Structures at Columbia University and the Daniel and Florence Guggenheim Laboratories at Princeton University.

Information concerning this fellowship should be obtained directly from the dean of the graduate schools at Princeton, Columbia and the California Institute of Technology.

The National Wildlife Federation

A limited number of graduate fellowships are awarded for study at an accredited college or university in the field of natural resources conservation. The fellowships have a value of $4,000.

For information, write the Executive Vice President, National Wildlife Federation, 1412 Sixteenth Street, N.W., Washington, D.C. 20036.

The Knights of Columbus Bishop Charles P. Greco Graduate Fellowships

This award was established for members, their wives, sons and daughters and widows and children of deceased members. The fellowships are for full-time graduate study leading to a master's degree in a program for the preparation of classroom teachers of the mentally retarded.

The fellowship, amounting to $500 a semester, is awarded for four semesters, upon evidence of satisfactory performance. The grant is renewable.

For information, write the Committee on Fellowships, Knights of Columbus, P.O. Drawer 1670, New Haven, CT 06507.

Foreign Area Programs

The Social Science Research Council and the American Council of Learned Societies offer a limited number of fellowships for training and doctoral research in social science and humanist fields related to specific foreign areas.

For information, write the Social Science Research Council, Fellowships and Grants, 605 Third Avenue, New York, NY 10016.

The National Science Foundation

In 1978, 500 graduate fellowships were awarded in all fields of science, including the social sciences, mathematics, engineering and interdisciplinary fields. The fellowships are for students of demonstrated ability.

For information, write the Public Information Branch, National Science Foundation, Washington, D.C. 20550.

The Center for Safety, New York University

Financial assistance in the form of fellowships is offered to candidates for the master's and doctor's degrees in occupational safety and health. The awards provide full tuition and stipends for full-time students and tuition support for part-time students. Applicants must exhibit interest in the field of occupational safety and health.

For information, write the Center for Safety, New York University, Washington Square, New York, NY 10003.

The deadline for applications is February 15 each year; awards are generally made in June for the academic year starting in the fall.

Dental Teacher Training Fellowships

These are available through a program established by the American Fund for Dental Health to develop more dental school teachers.

For information, write the American Fund for Dental Health, Attention: Mr. H. Kendall Beacham, Suite 1630, 211 East Chicago Avenue, Chicago, IL 60611.

The application deadline is February 1.

The American Congress on Surveying and Mapping

There are two fellowships for graduate students. The Keuffel and Esser Fellowship in Surveying and Cartography is worth $2,000, and the Wild Heerbrugg Geodetic Fellowship is worth $3,000. The deadline for application is January 15.

For information, write the American Congress on Surveying and Mapping, 210 Little Falls Street, Falls Church, VA 22046.

The American Association of University Women Educational Foundation

Fellowships are available to women who have completed all requirements for the doctorate except the writing of the dissertation. Awards are also made to women for postdoctoral research and for the final year of study in the fields of law, dentistry, medicine, veterinary medicine and architecture.

The value of the fellowships ranges from $3,500 to $7,000. Women who are citizens of the United States are eligible.

For information, write the Director of Educational Foundation Programs, American Association of University Women, 2401 Virginia Avenue, N.W., Washington, D.C. 20037.

20

Filling Out Financial Aid Forms

Processing financial aid forms is a necessary part of granting student aid.

Student Aid Has Allowed More Students to Go to College Than Ever Before

In the 1950s one out of five students pursued a higher education after high school. At the present time, the number of students attending institutions of higher learning may be one out of two.

Many parents hate to fill out financial aid forms. They ask us, "Why do we have to fill out these forms?"

The answer to this question is simple: you must fill out financial aid forms because the federal government requires it. Colleges expect parents to fill out the *Parent's Financial Aid Form* and the *Family Financial Statement*. The information on these forms tells the college how much your family will have to pay toward the cost of your education.

These forms are available at your local high school or the college of your choice. *You must fill them out if you want to get financial aid.*

Two firms who process these forms are:

1. College Scholarship Service
2. American College Testing Service.

How Do You Fill Out the Financial Aid Forms?

You must list your family's income, your family's assets, liabilities, dependents, etc. All the information on these forms is confidential and will be sent only to those colleges you indicate.

> *The forms should be completed as soon as possible after January 1 in the year you are applying for college.*

Is There a Fee for Filling Out a Financial Aid Form?

There are small fees for filing the FAF. At College Scholarship Service, it will cost $4.75 for the first institution and $2.50 for each additional college you indicate to receive the information. The fees are almost identical at American College Testing Service.

By paying a small fee, you can get a copy of the financial analysis which tells you how much your family has to pay. For the fee of $1.00 you know in advance what your family will be expected to pay for college expenses.

Where Do You Mail the Financial Aid Form (FAF)?

Instructions are on the form. Depending where you live, mail the completed FAF to:

> College Scholarship Service
> Box 2700
> Princeton, New Jersey 08540

> *or*

> Box 380
> Berkeley, California 94701

or you may mail the form to:

> American College Testing Service
> P.O. Box 1000
> Iowa City, Iowa 52240

Colleges may use one firm or the other. Therefore, you will have to find out which forms to use. It would be wise to check with your guidance counselor.

What Do These Firms Do with the Financial Aid Forms?

These firms look at your income, assets, dependents, and other things to decide how much your family can afford to pay toward the cost of attending college: *the Expected Family Contribution.*

How Do We Know Which of the Two Forms to Fill Out?

You can get help in this matter by consulting your guidance counselor or asking the Financial Aid officer at the college you are considering attending.

There are a few opportunities to attend Financial Aid Seminars. If you note that one is being held, encourage your parents to attend. It will be well worth their while in helping your family to better understand financial aid.

Once the FAF Forms Are Processed, the Financial Aid Director Decides What Financial Aid Package You Will Receive.

You can see that it is very important to fill out these forms. You may have to put in some time and effort right now, but later, when your student finds he has the financial aid money to attend the college of his choice, you will be happy you spent the time.

Generally, people feel that they know about how much they will have to pay toward college costs. In reality, the Financial Aid Form analysts seem to come up with a different figure of what a family can afford to pay.

Some examples of families of two parents, with one dependent child headed for college:

THE JAMES FAMILY

The James family has an income before taxes of $12,000 and assets of $10,000. Their son, John, is interested in seven colleges.

The amount this family will have to pay, according to the Financial Aid Form is $700. The college expects this student to save $500 from summer employment.

This is the way the Financial Aid Form Analysts arrived at the figure the family had to pay toward college costs.

Income before taxes	$12,000
Assets	10,000
John's summer job	500
Amount parents can pay	700
Amount family to pay toward education	$ 1,200

Now, let us consider another chart showing the colleges John is interest in, how much they cost to attend, the amount expected from the family, and the amount of financial aid that John will need to attend each university.

College	Cost	Expected from Family	Financial Aid Needed
Northern Florida Community College	$1,600	$1,200	$ 400
Florida A & M	1,800	1,200	600
Abraham Baldwin	2,200	1,200	1,000
Western Illinois	3,500	1,200	2,300
Michigan State	4,300	1,200	3,100
UCLA (Riverside)	5,600	1,200	4,400
Yale	8,000	1,200	6,800

If John attends Northern Florida Community College and gets no financial aid, he will have to pay $400. This chart clearly illustrates that without financial aid John will have trouble going to a more expensive college.

Without financial aid, attending Yale, UCLA, Michigan State or Western Illinois, would be out of the question if his family did not have some way to get approximately $600 to $6,800 to finance his college education.

Unless John could get a scholarship or loan or both, his best bet would be to enroll in Northern Florida Community College, Florida A & M or Abraham Baldwin College. Even then, his family would need to get extra money to pay for his education.

Clearly, it is to every student's advantage to know how much financial aid is available from the college of his choice. Your student can learn this by talking with the Financial Aid Director. He also needs to know how much money the family will be expected to contribute, according to the Financial Aid Form analysts.

THE SMITH FAMILY

The Smith family has an income of $17,000 before taxes and they have assets of $15,000. Their family consists of two parents and a daughter, Jean, who is headed for college. Jean is interested in the same colleges as John James.

The colleges Jean is interested in expect her to save $500 from her summer employment. According to the Financial Aid analysts, the Smith family will have to pay $1,300 toward the cost of Jean's college per year.

This is the way the Financial Aid Form analysts arrived at the figure the family has to pay.

Income before taxes	$17,000
Assets	15,000
Jean's summer job	500
Amount parents can pay	1,300
Amount family to pay toward education	$ 1,800

Next, let us consider a chart showing the colleges Jean is interest in. The chart shows how much they cost to attend, the amount expected from the Smith family and the amount of financial aid that Jean will need to attend each of these universities.

Jean can attend Northern Florida Community College and Florida A & M with no financial aid, according to the chart. At any one of the other colleges, the Smith family will have to get Financial Aid in the amount of $400 to $6,200, depending on the college that Jean selects.

College	Cost	Expected from Family	Financial Aid Needed
Northern Florida Community College	$1,600	$1,800	$ 0
Florida A & M	1,800	1,800	0
Abraham Baldwin	2,200	1,800	400
Western Illinois	3,500	1,800	1,700
Michigan State	4,300	1,800	2,500
UCLA (Riverside)	5,600	1,800	3,800
Yale	8,000	1,800	6,200

THE BROWN FAMILY AND SVEN BROWN

The Brown family has an income before taxes of $22,000 and they have assets of $20,000. There are two parents and their son, Sven. He would like to go to college with his friends Jean and John. He is investigating the same colleges listed in their charts.

Sven has a job this summer and the colleges he is interested in will expect him to save $500 toward his college education. According to the Financial Aid analysts this family will have to pay $3,200 towards Sven's college costs.

Income before taxes	$22,000
Assets	20,000
Sven's summer job	500
Amount parents can pay	2,700
Amount family to pay toward education	$ 3,200

College	Cost	Expected from Family	Financial Aid Needed
Northern Florida Community College	$1,600	$3,200	$ 0
Florida A & M	1,800	3,200	0
Abraham Baldwin	2,200	3,200	0
Western Illinois	3,500	3,200	300
Michigan State	4,300	3,200	1,100
UCLA (Riverside)	5,600	3,200	2,400
Yale	8,000	3,200	4,800

Sven can go to Northern Florida Community College, Florida
A & M, or Abraham Baldwin with no financial aid. If he goes
to Michigan State, he will need $1,100, UCLA $2,400, or Yale
$4,800.

THE WHITE FAMILY

The White family has an income before taxes of $27,000
and they have assets of $30,000. There are two parents and a
daughter, Marilyn, who is investigating the same colleges as John,
Jean, and Sven.

Marilyn has a summer job as a waitress. The college will
expect her to save $500 toward her college education. According
to the Financial Aid analysts, this family will have to pay $4,400
toward college costs.

This is the way the Financial Aid Form analysts arrived at
the figure the White family has to pay toward college costs.

Income before taxes	$27,000
Assets	30,000
Marilyn's summer job	500
Amount parents can pay	4,400
Amount family to pay toward education	$ 4,900

Let us consider a chart showing the colleges Marilyn is interested in, how much they cost to attend, the amount expected
from the family, and the amount of financial aid that she will
need to attend each university.

College	Cost	Expected from Family	Financial Aid Needed
Northern Florida Community College	$1,600	$4,900	$ 0
Florida A & M	1,800	4,900	0
Abraham Baldwin	2,200	4,900	0
Western Illinois	3,500	4,900	0
Michigan State	4,300	4,900	0
UCLA (Riverside)	5,600	4,900	700
Yale	8,000	4,900	3,100

The chart shows that Marilyn can attend five colleges without any financial aid. She needs $700 to attend UCLA and $3,100 to attend Yale. Of all the students, she seems to have the greatest choice of colleges she can attend with very little financial aid.

Even if you cannot find your family in these illustrations you can chart your own expenses once you know how much the Financial Aid analysts say your family will be expected to pay toward your college education.

What If My Family Income Changes?

If your family income goes up, your family contribution rises; if your family income goes down, the family contribution declines.

Does the Family Contribution Stay the Same?

The estimated family contribution will stay the same regardless of the cost of the college you attend. It won't make any difference if you attend a State University with a cost of $3,500 or a private college with a cost of $8,100.

What If My Family Is Different from the Examples you Give?

The larger the family, the less you will be expected to pay toward college costs. Other questions about this can be answered by the Financial Aid officer of the college of your choice.

Conclusion

Since student aid has allowed more students to go to college than ever before, your family should really think twice before refusing to fill out Financial Aid Forms. The forms are the only way that your family will find out how much they will be expected to pay toward the cost of your college education.

The Financial Aid Forms may be sent to either of two institutions: the American College Testing Service or the College Scholarship Service. Their financial analysts decide what you and your family will have to contribute toward your education costs.

In this chapter, we have chosen different families with varying incomes and assets. Does your family income and assets fit into any of these categories?

If not, check with the Financial Aid Director of the college of your choice to get a better idea of where you stand.

> *Remember, fill out financial aid forms early and accurately!*

21

How Student Aid Officers View
the Federal Aid Program

The paperwork that the federal government requires from the colleges to administer the federal program is driving student aid officers right up the wall!

The regulations of the Office of Education govern the way colleges and universities administer the federally financed student aid programs. The four programs regulated by the Office of Education are the Supplemental Opportunity Grant program, the College Work-Study program, the National Direct Student Loan program and the Guaranteed Student Loan Program.

The Office of Education demands so much paperwork that for several weeks we had to close the financial aid office at Rutgers University for a half day just to process all the forms.

When I was administering the Guaranteed Student Loan Program in Washington, I tried to involve the higher education community in the running of the program. I traveled throughout the country, visiting colleges, conferring with the ten regional commissioners of the program, explaining the new regulations and trying in every way to let the higher education community know that I was responsive to their feelings, that I hoped for their cooperation and that I would be available to anyone who telephoned.

Dallas Martin, executive secretary of the National Association of Financial Aid Administrators, recently spoke of the many new requirements. "I don't know what the Office of Education has in mind. Because the higher education community has not been as involved as it should have been, there are more problems than there ought to be."

When I took over as associate commissioner for Guaranteed Student Loans, I found that morale in the Office of Education was low. Former commissioners had resented the fact that the universities were displeased with the government's intrusion into academic affairs. Yet this was nothing new; many universities had felt this way. And I tried to point out to them that without the government's help many of them would go under.

Somehow the importance of cooperation with the federal government began to be realized, and we found the higher education community calling us in Washington when they had problems.

We found the banks to be more and more cooperative once they understood that our message was, we are here to help you, not to hinder you; we are available; call us!

My public relations director was a friend and an ally, and she helped in every way possible to bring this message home to the universities.

We established a hot line so that any university officer could dial us at any hour and get a recorded message about upcoming regulations and new laws. What I feared most was that I might fail in being cooperative with the higher education community, that I might become "inaccessible."

One of the most troublesome aspects of the current regulations involves the numerous records that institutions have to maintain for students who apply for and receive assistance from any of the government programs.

I believe that if you are going to administer a financial aid program, you must hire financial aid people to do it.

Unfortunately, the number of people in the Office of Education who have had college experience with financial aid programs is very small.

Education commissioners such as Terrel Bell and HEW secretaries such as David Mathews understood the college community and how it operated. They worked well with the academic community, and they were extremely likeable, capable men.

When it comes to the student aid programs, however, the

administration somehow gets carried away and hires people who are efficient but who do not understand aid operations at the college level.

Because of the way the Office of Education has set up its regulations, community colleges have a particular problem. Many of their students have nontraditional academic backgrounds, yet the colleges must show that these students are making "satisfactory progress" in order to get aid for them, and this simply may not be possible.

As assistant dean of students at a county community college in Detroit has explained, "At our school we have an open-door admissions policy. I don't know if we can ever expect our students to progress at any standard rate. The effect of the regulations will be to close the open door." And these are the students who may need the aid most!

Another regulation states that federal funds could be cut off to institutions where more than 50 percent of the students receive federally guaranteed loans either from banks or from the institutions themselves. In many cases, these are the very students who most need the aid.

An official in the Office of Education maintains that the only institutions that object to such requirements are "the less reputable, the less well-known" institutions. When I was financial aid director at Princeton, almost 50 percent of our student body received aid!

Even though the new student aid regulations have not yet been completed, campus financial aid officials are not happy.

One financial aid officer notes that by the time the regulations are completed, it will be time to begin the whole regulatory process all over again. (He refers to the new higher education bill that will come before Congress in 1981.)

Despite increases in the financial aid programs, there remain hundreds of thousands who still do not have enough money for college.

The Tax Credit Bill now being considered would make no appreciable dent in the cost of sending a student to college. The cost of college expenses is high and the figure involved here is small. Moreover, the money would not be received until the end of the year, and one needs money for college in the fall of the year, not at the end of the year.

Student aid expenditures for those who are worthy but who cannot afford to attend college need to be increased by at least $2 billion in the next few years.

It is my hope that when the new higher education bill comes before Congress in 1981, Congress will recognize that there are students who still cannot attend college—and will keep this figure in mind.

Index